To my new best friend –
John –

What a joy to meet
you – & see first-
hand what a W9-ATY-513
difference you are making
in the lives of so
many children –
You are a treasure!

Your friend,
8.5.05   Rmey

All the Difference

❧

*Tales in the life of a husband, a father,
a grandfather, a teacher and a storyteller...
and of those along the way who made all the
difference in his life.*

❧

By Riney Jordan

"All the Difference"

ISBN:0-9712069-1-0
Library of Congress Registration Number: TX-5-158-418
Second Edition, Jordan Publishing, August 2001
Printed in the United States of America

Riney Jordan Company
P.O. Box 867
Hamilton, Texas 76531-1937
254-386-4769
Fax: 254-386-4969
e-mail: riney@htcomp.net
Web: www.rineyjordan.com

❧

"Two roads diverged in a wood, and I —
I took the one less traveled by,
And that has made all the difference."

❧

From "The Road Not Taken" {1916}

—Robert Frost

Dedication

To my God, who has blessed me, sustained me, strengthened me, led me and loved me. Unless you've experienced Him, you can't possibly understand it. I'm sure I haven't always pleased Him, but He has never let me down.

To my wife, Karen, who has encouraged me in every endeavor of our married life for over forty years. Without her belief in me, this book would never have happened.

To my parents, Mr. and Mrs. Arthur Jordan, for caring so much about the right things, for giving me love so generously and things so sparingly. How blessed to be born into such a "wealthy" family.

To our three children, Le'Ann, Todd, and Sarah, who provided much of the inspiration. Hey, kids… have I told you lately how proud I am of each of you?

To our precious grandchildren. What joy Taylor, Caleb, Haley, Dustin, Annie, Luke & Anna Rose have already brought to us!

To my sister Shirley, who has always been an encourager, a friend, and a great source of material.

To Annell Todd, dear friend and confidante, who gave me the opportunity to write a monthly feature in her prestigious magazine, Texas School Business. Her encouragement, recommendations, and advice have truly helped make the difference.

To Vera Porter, extraordinary friend and public relations practitioner, who proofed the original manuscript and did so much to improve it.

To friends and members of the Texas School Public Relations Association for their encouragement, support, and friendship.

And to the following who have made such a difference in my life, in somewhat "order of appearance": Mrs. Z. T. Huff, Eddie and Bonnie Farren, Pat Davidson, Dorothy McIntosh, David Bartholomew, Mrs. Leota Bartholomew, Russell and Billie Jean Calhoun Dr. Mike Taylor, Brenda and Tony Eubanks, Warren and Charlotte Dearing, Bill Crabbs, Myra LaCasse, Annie Watters, Dorothy Bess Francisco, Mr. and Mrs. Bob Fail, Lynn Eggers, June Music, Roy and Joan Stewart,

Sonny and Frieda Rhodes, Tommy Taylor, Dr. Paul Jennings, Dr. Velma Walker, Mr. Walt Milner, Marion Brekken, Bobbie Fowler, Julia Mundheim, Dr. and Mrs. E. A. Sigler, The Honorable Gib and Sandra Lewis, Bob Massey, Dr. Jim Thompson, Junior and Mary Lou Crosby, Jack and Dona Kindle, Tom and Annette Joseph, and Jerry and Glenda Munson. All "friends for life."

Introduction

"Write a book?" I said. "I don't think it'll ever happen."

But the wife, who has far more vision than most futurists, kept insisting.

"You've got a book in you," she'd respond. "Several books, perhaps. Sit down, Riney, and write it. An hour a day, that's all it will take. And before you know it, you'll have it."

And, sure enough, what you're holding is the result. It comes about because of a loving wife who encouraged without nagging.

The title, *All the Difference*, came to me after much thought. So many people, including parents, relatives, teachers, friends, and students, have made such a difference in my life. I believe that we are the product of our association with others. Those changes come about through admiration, observation, and a desire to learn from them. Other people truly have made "all the difference."

Several of the chapters in the book first appeared as articles in the prestigious *Texas School Business* magazine. Annell Todd, editor, encouraged me by giving me the opportunity to pen an article a month. Many of you have indicated how much you would like to have some of the more popular ones in a collection. I hope you're not disappointed in my selections. By the way, *"A Tribute to Jesse"* received an Award of Excellence from the National School Public Relations Association.

What you'll find here are stories and incidents that have happened to our three children, and their children, and to the countless thousands of children who touched our lives everyday during my thirty years in public education. You'll find stories of my own childhood. And periodically you'll get my opinions on matters that mean so much to me.

It's also a look at how some things have changed, but how most things haven't really changed at all.

It's a glimpse into children and their feelings ... and they're not always pretty.

It's a means for us to laugh at ourselves, because laughter is such an important component for good health.

It's also an opportunity for me to give you some hope, the one thing so many teachers, parents, and students are lacking.

And, if I accomplish this, the book will have been more than a worthwhile effort.

Table of Contents

BONUS SECTION

All the Difference

1

The Beginning...
be it ever so humble

"Poverty keeps together more homes than it breaks up."

– H. H. Munro

The beginning. What a good place to begin. And I'm really tempted to begin with "It all began on a cold, dark rainy night," because I understand that it did.

It was the spring of 1942, April to be exact, and I came bouncing into the world at a whopping 10 lbs. 14 oz. in the delivery room of Shannon Memorial Hospital on a storm-filled Texas night in San Angelo.

My most notable feature at birth was that I had no hair. I grew it in later years, kept it for less than two decades, and then returned to my "newborn look" for the remainder of my days.

To say we were poor is not exactly correct. Like so many others during the years following the war, we were rich with the things that money couldn't buy: a storehouse of love, a vault full of understanding, and an indeterminate amount of care and compassion.

Looking back, I couldn't have had a better, more rewarding childhood.

Oh, we might have secretly yearned for more money, better cars, a nicer home, but in the long run, what we had, and what we didn't have, was helping shape character, and integrity, and faith.

As the Garth Brook's song says, "Some of God's greatest gifts are unanswered prayers."

I don't remember when Mom and Dad didn't work. Mother did everything you can imagine to make extra money. She took in ironing, she wrapped presents at Christmas time, she picked up pecans to sell, and she did some sewing. For several years she worked at the woolen mills running a loom. Hard work. Long hours. Little pay.

But she always did it with such an incredible attitude. She'd whistle and sing and make the very best of difficult times.

Dad, too, worked so hard. Times were tough, and he'd do anything to make some money.

When we moved to Brownwood in Central Texas in the late forties, he worked at a chicken slaughterhouse. It's difficult to imagine my Dad in such an environment, but he did it because it was the only job available. A few months later, a better job came along – working on the city garbage and trash route.

I remember once at the beginning of school in fourth grade, the teacher asked each one of us in class where our parents worked.

"My father works at the bank," one would say.

"My father owns the lumber yard," another would respond.

"My Dad drives a garbage truck," I innocently responded.

Laughter. Everywhere.

"What was so funny about that," I remember thinking.

That night, I asked my father about it.

"Daddy, why did they laugh?"

"Sometimes people see humor in the strangest things," he gently responded. "I'm so sorry that happened. In the future, if you're asked in public what your father does, you might just say that he works for the sanitation department. Maybe that will help."

And, as I would discover so many more times in my life, he was right.

I even found myself holding my head a little higher and with a little more pride each time I would say it. "He works for the city sanitation department."

My first lesson in public relations: *Presentation is everything.*

*Teacher said it. I believed it.
That settled it.*

"A teacher affects eternity;
he can never tell where his influence stops."
—Henry B. Adams

There's nothing quite like a teacher to make a difference in your life.

I'm convinced that most teachers don't begin to realize what an impact they can have on a child's life. In my case, I was blessed with a record number of gifted, caring teachers who each contributed significantly to the person I am today.

My first memories of school were in the little East Texas town of Elkhart. My teacher's name was Mrs. Salmon. Imagine what fun we had with that name! I remember learning to read using Dick and Jane books. I truly don't know if they used phonics, or word recognition, or rote memory. All I know is that I learned to read... and I loved it! Thank you, Mrs. Salmon, wherever you are. And, with a name like Riney, I should never have made a single comment about your name.

Second grade found us in the Texas German hill country town of Mason. This was the community my Dad had grown up in, and it was wonderful to have so many aunts and uncles around, speaking German on occasion, and always having freshly baked spice cookies and other delicious treats. Life here was ultra-conservative, and if you put something on your plate, you'd best eat it.

"There are children in China who are starving," my Uncle Jim would say. "Clean your plate."

Many of my childhood afternoons there were spent thinking of ways to package that leftover food and send it to them. I figured I'd be doing us both a favor.

My teacher for the first half of that year was Miss Ida Winkle. Everyone simply called her "Miss Ida." What an incredible lady. Not only did she strengthen my reading skills, but encouraged me in so many other ways. For example, there was a citywide art contest, and I'll never forget her coming over to me late in the afternoon as we were each finishing our entry.

As she knelt beside me, I remember her saying, "Your picture is so interesting, Riney. You are so creative and think of such creative ways to do things!"

I'd like to think of that as a compliment, although thirty years in the teaching profession have taught me that so often when teachers make that comment, it isn't always complimentary!

In the case of Miss Ida, however, I know that she meant it in the most encouraging way. But whether she did or didn't, I took it at full face value. And after that, whenever there was a project, I'd always think to myself, "Now how can I make this really different and really clever?"

There are so many more stories about my public school teachers and the other unbelievably influential people who made a difference in my life. But we'll save others for another day.

But now, it's time for a "homework assignment." Take a moment and write down the name of each teacher you had in your life. Hopefully you can remember most of them. Then, beside each name, list something you gained from having been in that classroom. You'll be amazed at the things you will remember!

And, you'll realize that you didn't get to where you are today all by yourself.

You are truly the product of the gifts of so many people who came before and gave so generously of themselves.

I once came across an old Korean proverb that said: "Power lasts ten years; influence not more than a hundred."

Who knows, even a hundred years may be an understatement.

3

Taffy and Chickens: A deadly combination

"*When all is said and done, monotony may after all
be the best condition for creation.*"
– Margaret Sackville

"**O**f course I know what I'm doing," I said. I probably rolled my eyes back and looked as indignant as I knew how.

Sister Shirley was right of course. I had no idea how to make taffy, but big brothers aren't supposed to let little sisters know things like that.

But… Mom and Dad were at work. It was summer. I was ten years old; Sister was eight. And we were bored.

So, it was on a hot July afternoon that I decided it would be great fun to make taffy, and to pull it, and then to eat it. Hey, if it turned out really good, we'd even share with Mom and Dad when they got home.

Out came the biggest pan we owned, and we started creating.

After all, as I've already told you, I had been "encouraged" to be creative. And this was going to be creative.

"Taffy is like candy," I deducted outloud. "So, we start with sugar. Taffy is kinda syrupy, too, so we'll pour in this bottle of syrup."

Let the cooking begin!

H-m-m-m-m-m. This didn't exactly look like the taffy we'd seen at the State Fair a few months ago.

"It needs flour to thicken it up," I announced. "I'm pretty sure taffy has flour in it."

One cup of flour. A little more. Oh, maybe two cups would be better.

"Most things have eggs in them," Sister Shirley offered.

"I know that," I lied. "Eggs were going to be the next thing I planned to put in. Give me two. No, make that three."

A little milk. A little water. A little this. A little that.

The more we cooked it, the darker it got.

Hey, must be time to pull it.

We poured it on a plate, and we tried to pick it up, but it wouldn't pull. It dripped. It ran. It stuck to us. But it wouldn't pull.

And the harder we tried, the less fun it became.

A quick look at the kitchen clock told us that it was time to begin cleaning up this mess.

But this was 1952 BD (before disposal), and from the looks of it, it wasn't something you'd flush either.

"Now what are we going to do," Sister Shirley whined.

"No problem," I responded confidently. "I know exactly what we're going to do with it."

Chickens. They'll eat anything. And I knew where there were scores of them, just a few hundred feet away in Dr. Hallum's backyard. I figured we'd do them a favor, and most assuredly, *us* a favor. Surely chickens liked something sweet, even if it didn't look like anything they'd ever seen before.

So, in a matter of moments, we were across the alley, leaning against the fence surrounding the chicken pen, scrapping out the pan, and letting the pieces fall where they might.

"What'd I tell you? Look how happy they are to get this," I said. "I bet they'll even be laying candy eggs in a couple of days."

Sister Shirley's face was all scrunched up and, without saying a word, it was obvious that she had serious doubts about this.

Within minutes, we were back in the kitchen, putting the finishing touches to the cleanup of our little experiment.

By the time Mom and Dad came home, even the aroma of burned sugar had disappeared from the house.

All's well that ends well.

❧

Two days later, Dad walked in the house from mowing the back yard. He had that concerned look on his face.

"Dr. Hallum's chickens have all died," Dad reported. "He can't figure it out, but said it was the strangest thing he'd ever seen. He believes they starved to death, because their beaks were all stuck together. Can you believe it? It's the darndest thing I've ever heard of."

Sister Shirley looked at me. I looked at her.

Well, I'm not proud of it, but it would be years before we would talk about it. And if there was ever anything that bonded me and Sister Shirley, it was the taffy.

Years later, I would be working at the local radio station, and for whatever reason, I would tell the story of the taffy to my nighttime audience.

"Dr. Hallum, if you're listening, I need to get it off my chest. I'm pretty sure it was our taffy that killed your chickens."

A few minutes later, a phone call.

"Riney, this is Dr. Hallum. I'm driving home and listening to you on the radio, and I've been laughing my fool head off. So *you're* the reason those chickens died. Well, if anyone ever did me a favor, you did! What do I owe you?"

Another happy ending. Another miracle. Another adult who understood that kids are going to make mistakes… and most of them *aren't* intentional.

Sure enough. All's well that ends well.

4

The Day Our Circus
Came to Town

❧

"There's a sucker born every minute."

—*P.T. Barnum*

You can blame Jimmy Roller for my interest in the circus. Jimmy was a neighbor of my best friend David and he lived down the street from David in an enormous white house with columns. Jimmy was several years older than David or I, and his backyard had become something that even Barnum and Bailey would envy.

Three rings. A trapeze from the tree. A costume and makeup area in the garage storeroom. Calliope music from the record player. And an imagination unlike anything you'd ever imagine.

He gave orders like General George Patton, and you didn't question him for one instant.

"Riney, you'll be a clown and also do a balancing act with the fishing pole."

"David, you'll be a clown, too, and you'll juggle two coke bottles."

"Carolyn, you're the trapeze artist. You'll wear your bathing suit when you perform."

Another was instantly transformed into a lion tamer. OK, so it was a "cat" tamer.

Another worked with the dogs. And, of course, Jimmy was always the ringmaster.

We took the circus to one of his friend's backyard for a birthday party, and the sawdust was in my blood after the one and only performance of Roller's Circus Cavalcade.

After that, I couldn't imagine a more exciting life. My favorite movie was "The Greatest Show on Earth." I must have seen it four or five times when it came to town.

When summer rolled around again, Jimmy was no longer interested in the circus. His interests are gone on into something else. So, I decided to become ringmaster of my own neighborhood circus: "Jordan's Greatest Show on 7th Street." It wasn't too original, but I felt good about it.

We didn't quite have the resources that Jimmy did, but old bricks served to lay out the circus rings. The hackberry tree was perfect for the swinging trapeze, and the storm cellar would be the dressing room. A large cardboard box served as the "tiger cage" to house the large alley cat that roamed the neighborhood.

David would be the clown, Linda Williams would be the animal trainer, Judy Raspberry would be the juggler, and Sister Shirley would be the trapeze artist.

I really needed Linda in the circus. Her father was the manager of the local RC Cola Bottling Company, and if we were going to be able to sell refreshments, I had to get at least two or three cases of RCs out of her.

And then the work began. The circus would be on the following Friday evening, so I hand printed posters and nailed them to every telephone pole in a three-block area. I made tickets, borrowed music and hung lights. To make the trapeze, I climbed the hackberry tree and hung a rope with a pipe threaded through it. I got one of Mom's best quilts and hung it across a wire in the cellar to make the girls a dressing room. I also brought a kerosene lamp from the house and put it in the cellar for light. It was perfect!

On the day of the circus, I was exhausted. We had practiced over and over. Shirley had swung on the trapeze from daylight until dark. We had nearly worn the record out practicing the grand entry, and I had drunk most of the RCs. About an hour before the circus, Mother stopped me and said, "Son, you look pale."

Faster than Tonto could say "You betcham'," I had a thermometer in mouth, Vicks Vaporub on my chest, and had swallowed a dose of Black Draught.

"But, Mom, I have to be the ringmaster. I can't be here in bed!"

"No problem. Announce through the window. It will be fine."

All the neighbors showed up, including Mrs. Johnson from across the street. She rarely came out of the house.

Everything started perfectly. The grand entry was just that: grand! David performed his clown act so well that Emmett Kelley would have noticed. And we sold the 14 remaining RCs in record time.

Almost before you knew it, it was time for our big finish.

"And now, Ladies and Gentlemen, our featured act of the evening," I shouted through the window screen. "Here's the one you've heard about: the death defying, incredible trapeze artist, Shirley, the Magnificent."

Well, she ate that up! She came out of the cellar, strutted around all three rings like she was the Queen of Sheba, and then jumped up on the trapeze. She had glued glitter all over her bathing suit, and she sparkled like a starlit summer night. The music started, and she began to swing back and forth, kicking her legs higher and higher with each swing. Just about the time you thought she could go no higher, one side of the pipe cut through the rope and Shirley the Magnificent went sailing through the air and landed squarely on her derriere.

The audience all gasped together as if on cue. Shirley's mouth was hanging open, and she looked almost comical as if she was wailing, and no sound was being made. Mother, of course, was there instantly, and as the reality of the death-defying act was realized, everyone surrounded her with more sympathy than the preacher could muster up during Mission's week for the "poor little children of China."

"She's all right, she's all right," I kept announcing. "Please take your seats. The show will resume in a few moments. Please be seated. She's all right."

"She's *not* all right, Riney," Mother announced as she looked at me as if I'd lost my mind. "I think her tailbone is broken."

When she finally got back from the emergency room late that evening, Mom asked, "Has anyone seen that patchwork quilt? I need it to put over Shirley."

"It's in the cellar, Mom. I used it for a curtain in the dressing room."

When she came back in the house a few minutes later, she gave me a look that would have melted an igloo.

"Did you put that coal oil lamp down there next to my good quilt," she asked.

"Uh, uh, I think so... uh, why?"

"Because the quilt got into the flame and there's only a neat little row of ashes across the cellar floor, that's why!" Mom said emphatically. "Your grandmother made that quilt!"

And that's how, in the summer of 1955, three important, life-changing events happened: Grandma's heirloom quilt was burned to the ground. A broken tailbone ended Shirley the Magnificent's career. And the circus that might have kept the bigtop alive, "Jordan's Greatest Show on 7th Street" ended its one-night stand.

5

The Day Heaven Smiled Down on Me Through a Sixth Grade Teacher

❀

*"No happy time is really gone,
if it leaves a special memory."*

—Author Unknown

I'll never forget the day I walked into her classroom for the first time. To say I was dreading sixth grade, would be an understatement. For years, I'd heard terrible stories about teachers, tests, and torture in sixth grade.

"Hardest grade you'll ever go through."

"It'll stop being fun now!"

"They pick only tough teachers for sixth grade. Have to. It's the only way they can control a sixth grader. Most of 'em are mean as the devil."

I wondered if he meant the students were "mean as the devil," or the teachers, or worst yet, perhaps both!

Needless to say, I didn't sleep a great deal during the week preceding the start of school. I'd almost convinced myself I was going to be asked to be put back into the fifth grade when I heard Mom say, "Get up. It's the first day of school."

Reluctantly I walked down the street to the elementary school about two blocks away. This enormous two-story building had never looked so threatening. We were all herded into the school auditorium on the second floor.

The first grade teachers read the names of their students, and once all of their classes were assembled, they left the auditorium.

Second grade teachers followed the same procedure. Then third and fourth. I prayed for my name to be called with the fifth graders, but it didn't happen.

A soft-spoken teacher, with radiant silver hair, walked to the front of the auditorium. She introduced herself as Mrs. Huff.

"First of all, boys and girls, let me assure you that everything you've heard about the sixth grade is not necessarily true. Those of us who teach sixth grade care so much about you and we want your time here with us to be meaningful, productive, and most of all, enjoyable! We are going to do everything we can to help you succeed. But, time and tide wait for no man, so let's get started."

"Time and tide wait for no man. H-m-m-m-m-m. Where did *that* come from?" I wondered.

Little did I know that I had just heard the first of many wonderful tidbits of wisdom from Mrs. Huff.

As she got closer to the "Js," my heart began to beat faster.

"Sheila Jackson."

"Present."

"Linda Gail Jones"

"Present."

Here it came. I prepared for the laughter, which inevitably followed the mispronunciation of my name.

Suddenly Mrs. Huff stopped. She gathered her thoughts for a moment. And then she looked up and smiled as she pronounced it correctly.

"Riney Jordan"

She looked straight at me and gave me a smile before I could even respond.

"Present!" I responded loudly. "Present!" And then I returned the smile.

Once the group was assembled, we followed her down the hall to her classroom. The view of the outside world was spectacular from our second floor classroom. But the view was nothing compared to the interesting and inviting classroom we entered.

There was a piano, and an easel and a reading corner. Famous paintings adorned the walls. Fresh flowers were on her desk. A science table housed an ant farm, wasp nests, bird nests, seashells, turtle shells, rocks, a microscope, pressed flowers, and science projects from previous years. The bubbling sound of a fish aquarium attracted my attention to the front of the room. A record player was softly playing something I would later discover was the work of a composer named Mozart.

As the days turned into weeks and the weeks into months, it was apparent that everything that I'd heard about sixth grade was wrong. I couldn't wait to get to school each day. Every morning, Mrs. Huff would read us a short story about honesty, or the value of hard work, or integrity or good citizenship.

And, yes, occasionally she would quote us a scripture.
Poor, dumb me.
I never knew my rights might be being violated.

6

Pottery, Poetry and Proverbs

"The secret of education is respecting the pupil."

—Ralph Waldo Emerson

L ife in Mrs. Huff's class was a new experience every day. Students were rarely absent for fear that they'd miss out on some of the fun.

She not only stressed the basics, but also incorporated them with art, music and drama. One of our major assignments each six weeks was to turn in at least six "creative" projects, such as a drawing, a poem, or a short story. She introduced us to pastels, watercolors, tempera, and ink. We experimented with clay and porcelain. Each semester, we had a study of a major opera. "Carmen," "Faust," and "Aida" became familiar to each of us.

The clay was of particular amazement to all of us. None of us had ever experienced anything quite like it. We would knead and shape and hone our objects, being reminded often to "get out all of the air bubbles."

"There's nothing worse than a piece of art that explodes in the kiln and ruins everyone's work," Mrs. Huff would caution us. "One bad apple can spoil the barrel."

H-m-m-m-m-m.

We were introduced to new terms like glaze, greenware, slip and firing. And as we would finish our objects d'art, Mrs. Huff would exclaim, "Oh, beautiful! Wonderful! Such a talent!"

"Remember, students, a thing of beauty is a joy forever."

The last few minutes of each day were spent reflecting on what we had learned. Then, Mrs. Huff would position herself at the piano and teach us songs you'd never hear on the radio.

My personal favorite was *When the Red, Red Robin Comes Bob, Bob Bobbin' Along*. I learned every word and would sing it at the top of my lungs.

> *"So wake up, wake up, you sleepy head,*
> *Get up, get up, get out of bed,*
> *Cheer up, Cheer up, the sun is red,*
> *Live, Love, Laugh and be happy."*
> *What if I've been blue?*
> *Now I'm walking through fields of flowers,*
> *Rain may glisten, but still I listen,*

For hours... and hours,
Cause I'm just a kid again,
Doing what I did again,
Singing a song!
When the red, red robin comes bob, bob, bobbing along!"

And then there were the others. *Just Whistle while You Work, Darktown Strutter's Ball, The Happy Whistler,* and *Camptown Races.*

Life was good in sixth grade!

From time to time, Mrs. Huff would talk about citizenship and what it meant to be an American. She'd tell us stories of men and women who had died in order for us to have the freedoms we enjoyed. We would learn of Iwo Jima and the Tomb of the Unknown Soldier and the Lincoln Memorial. As she told us about our heritage, she'd pass around old photos that had been carefully trimmed from old calendars and then pasted on construction paper.

"There's no place in the world like America," she would say. "Never take your freedom for granted."

And then we'd sing *"America,"* or *"The Battle Hymn of the Republic,"* or *"America the Beautiful."*

And more than once, we would watch and marvel as she played the piano and wiped a tear at the same time.

"America, America,
God shed His Grace on thee,
And crown thy good with brotherhood,
From sea to shining sea."

7

"Oh, to be a Dog Named 'Skillet'"

❦

*"Kindness in words creates confidence.
Kindness in thinking creates profoundness.
Kindness in giving creates love."*

—Lao-tzu

Each afternoon when school was over, it was one of our greatest joys to walk downstairs with Mrs. Huff and walk across that huge playground with her. She lived just across the street from the south end of the school, in what I thought was one of the biggest houses I had ever seen.

Years later, I would look at it and wonder what had caused it to become so much smaller than I remembered.

As we would approach the edge of the playground, her little squatty dachshund named "Skillet" would come racing across the yard, his underside barely clearing the ground. He'd jump around and let us all know that his owner and our teacher was someone who dearly loved him.

"Skillet, you're such a mess. Goodness, you've got to go on a diet!"

And then she'd slip him a treat.

And I thought to myself, "That is the luckiest dog in the world!"

8

A Simple Question That Changed My Life

"*The mediocre teacher tells.*
The good teacher explains.
The superior teacher demonstrates.
The great teacher inspires."

—Author Unknown

I was sitting at my desk working on an illustration for our classroom study of the opera "Carmen."

It was late in the afternoon and Mrs. Huff was walking around, admiring all the creative efforts of her "children."

As she stood alongside me, she knelt down and quietly said, "Riney, what do you plan to major in when you go to college?"

"Ma'am?" I asked.

"When you go to college, what do you plan to study?"

"I have no idea, Mrs. Huff. I haven't thought about it."

"Well, you know what I think you'd enjoy? Have you ever thought about becoming a teacher? You'd make a wonderful teacher!"

"Why, no. No, I haven't," I sputtered. "You mean, someday I might could do what *you* do?"

It seemed impossible to even imagine it!

"Of course, you could. You like school. You get along well with people. You like to read. I think you'd make a great teacher."

I was speechless. I was stunned. I was not even able to comprehend such a role.

She continued. "I like to envision my students as adults. I see them doing all sorts of things. Doctors. Lawyers. Nurses. Business owners. Musicians. They're all in here this afternoon, just waiting to be unleashed. Every one of us has a talent, a gift, and it's each of our responsibilities to try to nurture that gift, to make it grow, and allow it to fulfill our fondest dreams.

"Why, some of my former students are already grown and they're in politics, religion, education. But you, Riney, I see you teaching, influencing people. You'd make the classroom enjoyable, and exciting, and productive. You would make it relevant. You'd make it meaningful. You'd make it understandable.

"You'd make a difference."

I sat there in awe, trying to comprehend the bigger picture.

Influence? Difference? Meaningful?

Wow!

She bent over and gave me a reassuring hug. A huge smile came across her face.

"Yep. You'll understand it better someday. To teach means to share… to give. And we know it's always better to give than to receive. Don't we?"

9

*"Where there's a Will...
there really is a way!"*

"*For of sad words of tongue or pen, the saddest of these; it might have been.*"

—John Greenleaf Whittier

The day that Mrs. Huff suggested that I become a teacher was one of the most wonderful days of my life. It made me feel good. It made me want to do even better for her. It gave me hope.

I could hardly wait to get home and tell my parents. Dad always arrived home from the garbage route around 5:45. Mother had been home since around 3:30 that afternoon. Since Mom was cooking supper and Dad was watering the lawn, I decided to wait until we were all around the table to share my good news.

A typical supper at the Jordan household might be chicken fried steak, fried potatoes, fried okra and a big thick slice of homegrown tomato. It could have been fried salmon croquettes, mashed potatoes, black-eyed peas, and a big thick slice of homegrown tomato. But in all likelihood, most of the meal was fried.

And it was cooked in grease. Not shortening. Not corn oil. Grease. It was a combination of bacon drippings and lard. And that same "grease" had fried Sunday's chicken, the eggs every morning, and the potatoes each evening. It was kept in a crock on the stove, and no good Southerner with a lick of sense would have ever thrown it away after only one use.

Well, as we were sitting around the table, I humbly announced that Mrs. Huff had told me that she thought I would make a good teacher one of these days.

"Son, that is wonderful," Dad said. "What a compliment to you. I don't think we've ever had a teacher in our family."

"I know we haven't on my side, Son," Mom responded. "That Mrs. Huff is sure a sweet lady!"

"Well, what do you think?" I asked excitedly. "Would you like it? Wouldn't it be something! I think I'd make a good teacher. Why, we've been playing school for years, haven't we, Shirley?"

"*You* have!" Shirley said rather indignantly. "You're *always* the teacher and you always get mad cause I won't mind you. I don't think it's any fun, at all."

"Well, if you'd do the work like you're supposed to, I wouldn't get mad," I snapped.

"Now, kids. Settle down. Two wrongs don't make a right," Mom said.

"Son, nothing would thrill us more than for you to become a teacher. Why, that's one of the most honorable professions in the world. But, Son, did you know that if you're gonna be a teacher, you've got to go to college, and Son, college costs money. A lot of money. And your Mom and I don't have that kind of money."

"He's right, Son," Mom added. "He only makes about fifty dollars a week on the trash route and I make less than that out at the woolen mills."

"We'll think about it, Son. A lot can happen between now at the time you'd need to start. But I sure don't want you to get your hopes up and then it not happen because we couldn't afford it."

Dad looked almost apologetic at the thought of not being able to provide something as important as an education for his kids.

No one spoke a word for what seemed like an eternity.

Finally, Dad spoke. It was in that soft, gentle tone that was so much a part of him. "But, Son, Mother and Father always said something to me in German as a kid. In English, it was something like, 'If you want something bad enough, there's always a way to get there."

"Where there's a will, there's a way," Mom volunteered. "That's what my Momma always said."

"Goodness," I thought to myself. "That's what Mrs. Huff said. I guess Mom and Dad are more like teachers than they realize!"

❧

10

Encouragement: It's What a Teacher Does Best...

even for former students

❧

"The lessons of a great teacher will continue for a lifetime."

—Riney Jordan

As I walked into Mrs. Huff's classroom that morning, I was somewhat discouraged. I hadn't thought through the idea of becoming a teacher, and my excitement had caught my parents off-guard. Of course, they would love for me to get a college education and become a classroom teacher, but money was hard to come by, and it took every cent to pay the house payment, utility bills, and still have enough left over to feed the family.

What had I been thinking? I should've known you couldn't just be a teacher without going to some kind of school to learn how to do it. Now I'd worried my parents, set an impossible goal, and wished for something that was way out of my reach.

I guess I'd "gotten too big for my britches," as Mother always said about people who started acting "uppity."

Why hadn't I thought about how hard Mom and Dad have to work just to have what we've got? Didn't I remember that most of our clothes came from that trash route? I should be a whole lot more thankful than I was. A lot of kids didn't have the luxury of having their Dad bring something home almost every day.

And the best part: It was always free.

"People throw away perfectly good stuff," Dad would say.

His folks were full-blooded Germans. Dad had grown up in the Texas hill country around Mason, Texas. His father was an old-fashioned, Bible-believing Methodist minister who pastored the German Methodist Church in the little German settlement of Art, Texas. The old sandstone building is still there today, only now with a Texas historical marker.

My great-grandparents had come to Texas in the mid-1800s from Germany as part of the Peter's Colony. They arrived in the winter at Galveston, Texas and many of them didn't survive the harsh cold months.

As they gradually moved north, many of my ancestors settled in central Texas around Fredericksburg, Llano, Fort Mason, Castell, and Pontotoc. These were a conservative, God-fearing people who worked hard, loved their families, and treasured many of the old ways.

Dad was the only one of his eight brothers and sisters to ever leave Mason County. The rest were born there, lived there, worked there, worshipped there, and died there.

I was sitting there starring out the window, imagining my father's life as a child, when Mrs. Huff walked over and quietly asked, "Is everything alright, Riney?"

"Oh, sure," I quickly responded. "I... I... was...uh... just thinking about what my father said last night. I'm probably not going to get to be a teacher because we can't afford it."

There... I had said it! I hadn't meant to share the fact that my parents couldn't afford it, but I had, nevertheless.

Mrs. Huff knelt down, put her arm around me and looked me right in the eye.

"Riney, you know your parents would love for you to have a college education, but it's difficult for almost any family to pay for a college education. Don't worry about that right now. In the meantime, study hard, learn everything you can, and go on dreaming about being a teacher.

"I just want you to remember that if you want something in life, go for it. Dream big. Use your God-given talents and do something in life you love. A job ought to be fun, enjoyable, and make you feel like you've helped someone along the way.

"There's nothing sadder than someone who goes to work everyday and hates what they do, so don't ever get caught in that trap.

"If you want to teach, then become a teacher. Oh, of course, you may have to do without some things that other kids have, but believe me, it'll be worth it.

"Just remember: Where there's a will, there's a way!"

Sixth grade ended much too quickly that year. Before I knew it, the hot days of late May were upon us, and we were cleaning out our desks and the "cloak" room in preparation for summer vacation.

"Oh, I'm going to miss everyone of you," Mrs. Huff said to us on her final "sermon."

During the course of the year, some of the kids jokingly referred to her as our sixth grade "preacher." Often times on the playground, a group of youngsters would gather around Mrs. Huff and chant, "We got us a preacher, not a sixth grade teacher."

Mrs. Huff would throw her head back and laugh.

"You'll appreciate me some day," she'd say.

On this her final lesson, she talked to us about doing our best, about loving our country, about being good citizens. She told us to dream our dreams, then work hard for them. She reminded us that "a rolling stone gathers no moss" and that the Golden Rule would always work for us. She told us she loved us, and at that point, I would swear I saw a tear swell up in her eye.

And then she said: "And kids, come by the house and see me this summer."

"Why not?" I thought.

Mrs. Z. T. Huff. What a teacher!

❧

I'm not sure what prompted me, but one day that summer I walked the three blocks to the neighborhood grocery store and noticed Mrs. Huff's house across the street.

"Maybe I'll stop by for a short visit," I thought to myself.

Little did I realize that it would be the first of many such visits during the weeks and months ahead. Mrs. Huff invited me to help clean out her storeroom alongside her garage one Saturday. Another day I helped her pour slip, liquid clay, into some of her ceramic and porcelain molds. One day might be spent cleaning one of the many aquariums in her sunroom. Or I might help her work in the flowerbeds outside their beautiful rock home.

But each visit would acquaint me with another interesting facet of her life. She'd pull a hardbound book from her library shelf and say something like, "Here, Riney, any well-educated person needs to know about David Copperfield. I think you'll like it."

Her favorite paintings were of the old masters. I remember prints of Gainsborough's "The Blue Boy" and Thomas Lawrence's "Pinkie" occupying a prominent place in the formal living room. She would often play music on the small grand piano, which was at one end.

Once, she hired me to make a "formal phone call" to everyone she wished to invite to a garden party at their home.

All of the men were to be addressed as "Master" and all of the women as "Madam." It was all scripted for me, and I've often thought how amusing it must have been to the recipients to hear a child's voice reading such a sophisticated announcement.

As time progressed, I would see Mrs. Huff at various locations around town. She never failed to ask, "Are you still interested in becoming a teacher? You'd make a good one!"

Once she gave me a call and indicated that she was going to be cleaning out her "cupboards" that following weekend, and she was going to have all sorts of teacher magazines, books, and teacher supplies.

"Would you like to have them? I immediately thought of you," she said. "Why don't you come down and pick them up? I'll have them in boxes for you."

I drug the boxes the four blocks to my modest home and pushed them under the bed. Every night I would read those old *Instructor* and *Grade Teacher* magazines and dream of the day when I would have my own classroom. Many a night I went to sleep with a book or magazine on my chest.

During the high school years, it was not uncommon for Mrs. Huff to call and ask if I would be interested in grading some papers for her. "I'll pay you, of course," she'd say, "but I think it would be good experience for you.

"Just be sure to write encouraging words to the students," she'd add.

The night I graduated, Mrs. Huff was there. After the ceremony, she came up and gave me her usual big hug, and beamed as she proclaimed, "Now you can begin college to earn your teaching certificate. I'm so excited!"

"Oh, Mrs. Huff," I said. "I can't wait either, but it will be at least a year or two before I have enough money saved up in order to enroll."

"Well, in the meantime," she said, "I want to take you next week to meet some folks I know. What are you doing Monday afternoon?"

"Why, why nothing really," I stammered. "Where are we going?"

"You'll see," she said.

And she had a grin on her face as broad as the quarter moon that hung in the sky on that summer eve.

❧

Promptly at two o'clock on the following Monday, she pulled up in front of our small two-bedroom frame house in a large white Cadillac.

Somewhat reluctantly, I ran and jumped into the front seat.

After polite greetings, I quizzed her about our outing.

"Oh, just a simple little visit with some folks," she said.

And she immediately changed the subject.

We drove for several blocks, turning right, then left, then right again. Before I knew it, she pulled alongside the curb in front of what everyone knew as "Old Main" on the Howard Payne College campus.

"Mrs. Huff, please, what are we doing here?" I begged. "I can't possibly enroll yet. We're just here to get information, right?"

At that moment she turned, looked me right in the eye, and said, "Riney, ever since you were in my sixth grade class I've encouraged you to become a teacher. You've indicated that you'd like that, too, so today, we're going to meet some people who might be able to help you.

"There are several things in your favor. For example, you made good grades in high school. That's good. You have a part-time job. They'll like that. They like to see students working hard for something as important as an education. I also want to check on scholarships while we're here. Many of them go unclaimed every year because no one even applies.

"And there is one more thing you might not realize is in your favor today. You see, my husband is vice president of the college, and I don't think that will hurt anything!"

I was speechless. Stunned. In shock.

She got out. I realized that I was still sitting, with my mouth hanging open, so I quickly joined her on the sidewalk.

And that day, I walked down the longest sidewalk I'd ever seen, up the tallest steps I had ever taken, with my sixth grade teacher. She was still guiding me, still teaching me, still encouraging me, even after all these years.

Before the afternoon was over, I was enrolled in the education department of Howard Payne College, Brownwood, Texas.

A few years later, I would graduate at mid-term with a Bachelor of Science degree and would accept a fifth grade teaching position in Grapevine, Texas, located north of Dallas-Fort Worth.

At the end of my first full-year of teaching, my peers selected me as their representative for the district's "Teacher of the Year" program.

At my first Chamber of Commerce banquet, I heard a bio being read which sounded very much like my own, and a few minutes later, I heard them call my name. I walked to the podium to receive the award for Grapevine-Colleyville ISD's "Teacher of the Year."

And for one of the few times in my life, I was speechless.

❧

11

One Last Lesson from an Old and Trusted Friend

"Many people have gone a lot farther than they thought they could because someone else thought they could."

—Zig Ziglar

I kept in touch with Mrs. Huff for several years. Each call was equivalent to another lesson from this master teacher.

Often I would ask her advice about a student who was having difficulty. She always gave the best advice. Generally, she recommended that I visit with the child and get to know him a little better.

"Nothing can ever take the place of improving a relationship," she would say.

Mrs. Huff eventually retired from teaching and I found myself contacting her less and less.

As many of you know, time has such a way of getting away from us. Weeks turn into months, months into years, and before you know it, you realize that you haven't visited with an old friend in years.

Several years later, I received a call from Mom.

"Son," she said, "I needed to let you know about Mrs. Huff. Did I ever tell you that her husband passed away, and that they've diagnosed her with Alzheimer's?"

As the conversation continued, I listened in stunned silence as I learned that Mrs. Huff had been placed into a nursing home facility and that a recent stroke had left her virtually speechless.

"Son, you really ought to come home as soon as you can, and go out and visit with her for a little while. I thought you might want to thank her one more time for everything that she did for you.

"We're not sure how much longer she's going to be with us," Mom added.

"Of course, Mom," I replied. "We'll see you on Saturday."

When I hung up the phone, I sat down and visualized the vibrant, enthusiastic, caring individual I'd known simply as Mrs. Huff. It seemed impossible that someone with so much energy and love for life could ever be contained in a nursing facility.

She'd always given so much to so many, and it was difficult to imagine her in a situation where she was unable to help herself.

As the weekend drew nearer, I thought a great deal about what to say. Would it upset her for me to relive such wonderful moments? Would she even remember me? Would I be able to convey the depth of my appreciation for her in a brief visit?

In spite of the questions, I knew one thing for sure: I needed this visit perhaps even more than she did. I had to see her, thank her, hold her hand just one more time.

On Saturday morning, Karen and I loaded the kids into our car and drove the two and a half-hours back home. When we arrived at my parents at mid-morning, everyone agreed to stay there while I drove out to the nursing home by myself.

As I walked into the door of the nursing home, the mixed smells of body waste, medicine, and bland food hit me immediately.

"Mrs. Huff would never fit into a place like this," I thought. "She has far too much dignity to be here."

But as I quickly scanned the room for a receptionist area, I spotted her sitting in a wheelchair, looking out one of the few windows in the place.

I paused a moment and looked at the beautiful silver hair that I had remembered as a child.

"Why, she hasn't changed that much at all," I thought.

As I slowly walked toward her, I noticed that she had lost a bit of weight, and she was wearing a simple, cotton print dress. She had a slight smile on her face as she studied the beauty of the outdoors.

I knelt down beside her and patted her gently on the shoulder. She looked around, the smile still on her face, and reached over and patted my hand that was resting on the arm of her chair.

"Mrs. Huff, how are you?" I asked.

My words were slow and deliberate, and a bit louder than usual.

"You probably don't remember me, but I was a former student of yours in the sixth grade. You were such a wonderful teacher, and you did so much for me. I ... I... uh... just wanted to stop by and thank you for being one of the most precious people I've ever known."

I felt tears welling up in my eyes, and I didn't want her to see me get emotional. That would likely upset her, too, I assumed.

She continued smiling, tried to say a few words, but the stroke had cruelly removed her ability to be understood.

"It's O.K. Don't try to talk. I just wanted to stop by and tell you that I will never forget you as long as I live. You used to invite me down to your house to help clean out your aquariums. And you taught me how to do ceramic and porcelain pieces. I remember so many times when you would give me teaching materials because you told me that I would be a good teacher someday."

My mind was going faster than the lead car at an Indy race. I recounted the opera units, the artwork, the spelling bees. I told about visiting her home at Halloween and being in awe of her in a witch's costume, stirring a cauldron of water and dry ice. I recalled listening to her read great children's stories to us each afternoon after lunch, repeated some quotes she said so often to teach us values, and remembered the wonderful, uplifting songs we would sing late in the afternoon.

"I remember singing *Darktown Strutter's Ball* and *The Happy Whistler* and my favorite was always *When the Red, Red Robin Comes Bob, Bob, Bobbin' Along.* Do you remember, Mrs. Huff? Do you remember?"

She looked deep into my eyes, and continued smiling.

"I loved hearing you play the piano," I quickly added. "Do you, uh, do you… uh, still play the piano?"

Immediately I thought to myself, "What a stupid question! You idiot, of course she can't play the piano in this condition!"

But instantly, her face lit up. A huge smile came on her face. She began pointing across the room with short, quick, jerky motions that indicated her excitement.

I turned and noticed an old up-right piano across the room.

"Do you still play the piano?" I asked in amazement.

Her head nodded quickly up and down as she continued to point to the piano.

"Would you like for me to move you over there?"

Again her head nodded excitedly.

I moved behind her chair and rolled it across the room to the piano. Once the bench was out of the way, I moved her within inches of the keyboard, and her fingers immediately began dancing across the black and white ivories.

The first song of the concert? *When the Red, Red Robin Comes Bob, Bob, Bobbing Along.*

The music began to lift the spirits of everyone in the room. Old men and old women turned toward the source of the music and every face was wearing a smile.

She was still bringing joy after all these years!

When the concert ended, she looked up at me with an open smile and a twinkle in her eyes.

"Wonderful! Just wonderful!" I told her.

I knelt down again and shared a few more thoughts. About the encouragement. About graduation. About her help in getting me enrolled in college. About being such an influence in my life.

"You aren't sure who I am, are you?" I asked.

She smiled, and for just a moment, I think I saw a flicker of recognition of students and faces and of days long since gone. For just a moment I felt that she saw herself back in that second-story classroom at South Ward School across the street from her home on Seventh Street. For just a brief moment, she went back.

But then she smiled, and her eyes glistened, and she slowly, sadly, looked at me, and began shaking her head slowly from side to side.

"Mrs. Huff, my name is Riney Jordan. I became a teacher, just like you suggested, and it was one of the best decisions I ever made. But, Mrs. Huff, it would never have happened had it not been for you.

"Thank you. Thank you from the bottom of my heart."

I gave her a gentle hug, kissed her on the cheek, and rose to leave.

She slowly reached up, took my hand with one of hers and slowly, lovingly patted it with her other.

🌹

As I drove slowly back across town, I couldn't help but think about how fortunate I had been to be a student of Mrs. Huff. She was, in my mind, the benchmark of a master teacher.

She not only taught me reading, she also taught me respect.

She not only taught me math, she taught me manners.

She not only taught me how to learn, she taught me how to live.

And after this visit, she taught me how to close out a full life with dignity and honor.

Mrs. Huff died a few months after my visit. I don't doubt that she still had that soft, gentle smile on her face.

I also have no doubt that the first words she heard as she entered the heavenly realm, were these:

"Well done, my good and faithful servant."

All the Difference

12

And This Has Made
All the Difference:
A Tribute to Jesse

❧

"There is not a man that has not 'his hour,' and there is not a thing that has not its place."

— *Ben Azzai*

Let's face it. Some things really are better now than they "used to be."

I was fresh out of college in mid-year and had accepted my first teaching assignment. And what emotions were running through my head as I walked into that classroom for the first time at the start of the second semester in 1967. Thirty-two fifth grade students were sitting there, looking straight at me, and I remember thinking, "They have the same look of fear and uncertainty on their face as I do."

The one thing that struck me as I surveyed the room was the tremendous diversity of the students. Some looked *very* young, and some looked almost as old as I was. Some were dressed as if they were in high church, while others were dressed almost comically, with dingy colors and nothing coordinated. A few of the girls had ribbons in their hair, yet others had long hair that appeared as if it had never been washed or combed.

As the day progressed and I began to match names in a grade book with faces, I suddenly noticed what appeared to be another adult in the room walking to the pencil sharpener. He had been sitting in the far back corner of the room and hadn't spoken or participated all morning. As long as he was seated, you didn't realize his size. But goodness he was tall! As I watched this lanky, six-foot tall student saunter around the back desks, I noticed that his jeans were too short, the shirt had been patched, and long, unkempt hair hung in his face. Through the process of elimination, this had to be Jesse.

In the days and weeks ahead, I learned a great deal about Jesse. He had just turned sixteen years old and was repeating fifth grade for the second time. He hadn't started to school until he was seven, and he had also been retained in first grade and third grade. I discovered that one reason I was hired was because all the women teachers were afraid of him. Some talked about rumors of a knife he always carried, and others told of fights off campus with other teens.

It didn't take long to realize that Jesse had two major problems: 1) He couldn't read and 2) His self-esteem was as bad as it gets.

I worked diligently with him on both, but major repairs require major investments. We met before school, after school, during lunch but progress was ever so slow. The material was of no interest to him and he frustrated easily. But he kept telling me over and over, "I really want to learn to read, Mister Jordan, but it's so hard." And then he'd smile. "But we'll make it, won't we?"

His parents came to open house during Public School Week that spring. Here were two of the most humble, precious people I'd ever met. In their most gracious manner, they thanked me for the extra effort I was making with Jesse.

Looking at me with the darkest saddest eyes you could imagine, his father told me that neither he nor his wife could read, they spoke little English, but, more than anything, they wanted their children to learn to read. Nothing was more important to them! And, as they left, Jesse's mother, who never said a word, reached into her purse and handed me a foil-wrapped package of homemade flour tortillas.

They had so little but wanted to give so much.

The end of school came much too quickly that year. Jesse had made some progress, but still had a long way to go.

He gave me a hug and that trademark smile as he went out the door for the last time, and looked me right in the eye and said, "You're a good teacher, Mr. J."

In the years that followed, I heard very little about Jesse. He dropped out of school the following year, and went to work at a warehouse near his home. Once, I ran into him at the grocery store, and he told me about his wife and new baby. Family meant a great deal to this middle-school dropout.

Jesse was one of those students you never forget. They are fixed in your mind just as carvings, which are etched into stone. They're permanent. They don't go away.

Years pass. Things change. And when you're least expecting it, that one-in-a-million chance encounter occurs, and your life will never be the same.

Almost thirty-years later, in my last year of working in the public schools, I am serving as principal of an elementary school. It's the first day of my last year. Parents, and kids, and teachers are everywhere. It's that chaotic 30-minute period on the first morning.

I look up just long enough to notice what appeared to be an older looking gentleman walking in the front door. His walk is slow and he is uncertain where to go or what to do. He is holding the hands of little twin girls who looked like they were going to their first christening. Ribbons were in their hair. The shoes were sparkling. New supplies were under their arms. This is an important day in their life and they've been anticipating it, preparing for it, and yearning for it for months.

As I make my way toward them, I'm interrupted several times with greetings and questions. As I reach them, the gentleman's face breaks into a big smile, and he extends his hand of greeting.

"Mister Jordan, Do you remember me? My name is Jesse. Jesse Sustaita. Do you remember me? You taught me how to read when I was in your class in fifth grade. Remember?"

I didn't want the moment to end. I looked at him and reached into the depths of my mind for that first time I had met Jesse almost thirty years ago. Oh, he still had the same dark hair, only now with beginning shades of gray. Those long slender fingers were rough and weathered. The jeans that he always wore had been traded for coveralls. But the eyes and the trademark smile were the same.

He introduced me to his granddaughters. They had inherited that trademark smile.

"You'll take care of them, won't you, Mr. Jordan? You'll teach them to read, won't you?" Jesse pleaded. "I brought them today so they could meet *my* teacher."

"Don't doubt it for a minute, my friend. We'll not only teach them how to read, we'll also love them!"

With that, he smiled, handed me their lunch boxes, reached into his pocket, and pulled out a small foil-wrapped package.

"Tortillas," he said. "My wife and I made them especially for you this morning. Thank you, Mr. J, for caring."

Déjà vu.

And before either of us could even consider how it looked, we embraced.

Sometimes a hug can speak volumes about how much you care for a person.

Jesse told me that he needed to get to work.

"Their mom and dad will by this afternoon to get them. Would you mind taking them the rest of the way?" he asked.

And as I walked Jesse's granddaughters to their kindergarten classroom, I turned and nodded once more at my friend, Jesse. Once again, he gave me that classic smile from ear to ear.

These two precious little girls had so much... and their future had never looked brighter.

13

Hey Buddy, Can You Spare a Dime?

"There, little luxury, don't you cry — you'll be a necessity by and by."
—Author Unknown

I loved teaching. And those fifth grade students were so much fun! The wife used to get quite amused when one or more would stop by our house after school and ask, "Can Mr. Jordan come out and play?"

Although we didn't realize it perhaps as much as others, obviously we were quite poor at the time. My starting teaching salary was around six thousand dollars a year, and with two toddlers at home, it was our only income.

The school district, however, was so good to us. The first Monday of summer vacation, I got a call from the Superintendent.

"Riney, I'd like for you to be the counselor this summer for the Head Start Program. It pays six dollars an hour, lasts from 8:00 a.m. to noon, and we feed you lunch."

Head Start, designed for low-income preschoolers, would last until mid-July. I explained to him that I would love to do it, but that I didn't have a counseling degree and that I didn't know one thing about it.

"You don't have to know anything about counseling," he snapped. "Heck, did you ever meet a four-year-old who needs counseling? This is one of those government programs. What do they know about what kids need?"

So, with that phone call, I could now add "counselor" to my résumé.

I must admit that this was one of the most enjoyable jobs I ever had. I'd play with the kids during recess, I'd read to them, I'd answer their questions, and I'd have lunch with them.

And what lunches they were! I was accustomed to regular school lunches, but since it was government funded, we ate good! Fried pork chops, watermelon slices, corn on the cob, and apple pie were routine fare. I must admit that I felt a little guilty eating such elaborate lunches while Karen and the kids were home having Vienna sausage and canned ravioli.

Each Friday was field trip day. We loaded onto a school bus and one week visited a farm, the next week a fire station, and then the police station. One week we took the children to the zoo.

But none of these stand out as much in my memory as the Friday we drove to Dallas to Love Field to visit the airport.

Few, if any, parents were able to go with us on these Friday jaunts, so generally, the bus driver and I were the only men along, and he stayed with the bus while we "toured."

As our visit to the airport was coming to a close, Mrs. Dawson, the director of the program, announced that we would take a bathroom break prior to reloading on the bus.

"Mr. Jordan, would you take all the little boys and supervise them?" she asked.

"Sure. Come on, guys. Line up behind me and we'll take care of this."

When we entered the restroom, the little guys immediately headed for the urinals. Almost immediately, one said, "I'm too short. I can't reach it."

H-m-m-m-m-m. He did have a problem, and so did *all* the others, I quickly observed.

"No problem. Just line up behind me and I'll lift each of you up high enough for you to go."

You may not believe this, but a fifty-pound little fellow can seem like a hundred pounds if you have to hold him for very long. And after two or three had completed their business, I was working up a sweat and time was running out.

"Hold it," I announced. "Let me think about this."

I looked around the partition where the toilets were located.

"Hey, just use these. They're regular toilets like you have at home. Come on around and use these."

The first child who tried to pull open the door announced, "Mr. Jordan, they're all locked!"

Upon closer examination, I realized that they were *pay* toilets, and each one required a dime. Now remember, I'm only making about six thousand dollars a year, and I rarely had any money in my pocket, much less fifteen to twenty dimes to poke into toilet doors. I reached into my pocket and found a nickel and a few pennies.

H-m-m-m-m-m.

Suddenly it came to me. Why, there's a crawl space under each door. These guys are small enough. They'll fit under there with no difficulty at all. What a genius!

"Hey, *I* don't have any money, and *you* don't have any money, and *we've* got a problem, and *I* know what we can do. Just get on your tummies and crawl under the door, take care of your business, and crawl back out. OK? Let's go!"

I must tell you that they did this assignment with all the gusto in the world. They were giggling and scooting and this plan was working great!

About this time I noticed one little guy crawl under about halfway, then scoot back out.

"Wait till the one before you is finished and out before you crawl under," I announced.

A few minutes later, I observed the same thing again at the same stall.

H-m-m-m-m-m. One of these youngsters is taking entirely too long in there.

As I started toward the stall, I raised my voice and said, "We're in a big hurry, guys. Take care of your business, then scoot out. Now someone in *this* stall is taking entirely too long!"

At this moment, I raised up on my tiptoes to peer over into the door to see who was causing this delay.

"Now your time is up. I need you out of there right now!"

As I peered over the top of the toilet door, I wasn't prepared for what met my eyes. Here was the largest man I had ever seen, sitting on the toilet, reading his newspaper.

For just a moment I was speechless! But I felt I owed this man an explanation as to why every few minutes a little four-year head was popping under the door, starring up at him between his feet.

"Uh... uh... Oh, I am *so* sorry. Please, let me explain. You see, I'm with the Grapevine-Colleyville School Distr...."

"Mister, I don't really care where you're from. Just go away!" he glared.

"Of course, uh, no problem…. I'm sorry…."

At a time like this, are there really words in the English language to adequately express your sentiments?

Shortly after this incident, I read in the *Dallas Morning News* where the decision had to been made to eliminate pay toilets at Love Field.

Just my luck! A day late… and a dime short.

14

To Pray or not to Pray?
That's not a question!

"*The trouble with being an atheist is you have nobody to talk to when you're alone.*"

—Author Unknown

I've never been so confused in my life.

Just about the time I think I know what the Supreme Court meant in its school prayer decision, the issue is in the news again.

Now can I pray in school? Can a student pray in school? Do I have to be a student, or act like one, to be able to pray? Frankly, I think it's still between the Man and me.

I remember years ago when someone so wisely wrote, "as long as there are tests in school, there will be school prayer."

I also remember someone saying "that the trouble with being an atheist is that when your motorcycle plunges off a cliff into the Colorado River and you aren't killed, there's no one to thank."

Well, maybe it's time to thank God for the things that *didn't* happen this past year in our schools.

I'm thankful the vast majority of our students made it safely to school every day.

I'm thankful that thousands of busses everyday, loaded with the most precious cargo known to man, made it through morning and afternoon traffic, around hairpin curves, down lonely country roads, and even in the dark of night, and they made it without a hitch.

I'm grateful that teachers all over the world loved their students for all the right reasons, and that they worked tirelessly to teach curriculum *and* compassion.

I'm thankful that in almost every case, school board members voted to do what was best for children.

I thank God that far more parents did a remarkable job of parenting than those who didn't.

I'm grateful that over 98% of our students didn't commit a major crime this past school year.

I'm thankful that most of our students care about their education, their fellow students, their teachers, their parents, and their country.

I thank God that He was there for countless thousands of students when they were left home alone, when they walked home after school, when they crossed busy streets, when they played in parks.

I'm thankful that most schools didn't have a major crisis this year... that most schools didn't have a major accident this year...

that most schools didn't grieve over the loss of a child… that most schools didn't have an employee who abused a child… that most schools didn't decline on academic tests.

I'm thankful for every day in our schools when negative news doesn't occur.

I'm thankful for every day that teachers work together for the betterment of youngsters. I'm thankful for every hour that parents and school members sit down and determine the best route for children. I'm thankful for every second that students enjoy being in school.

A little kindergarten girl reportedly told God in her prayer that she was confused. In school, she learned that Thomas Edison made light. In Sunday school, they said God made light.

"He stoled your idea, didn't he?" she remarked.

Aren't we thankful for their insights!

I'm also thankful that someone recently slipped me a copy of a prayer that works for every one of us, everyday.

This is the beginning of a new day. God, you have given me this day to use as I will. I can waste it or use it for good. What I do today is important, because I'm exchanging a day of my life for it. When tomorrow comes, this day will be gone forever, leaving something I have traded for it. I want it to be gain, not loss; good, not evil; success, not failure, in order that I shall not regret the price I paid for it.

So, as many of you relax a bit during the summer months, be thankful.

When you return in the fall, be thankful.

When you work diligently to make this world a better place for children, be thankful.

When you have time to spend with children, be thankful.

Six-year old Elliott once wrote a letter to God that read: "Dear God, I think about you sometimes even when I'm not praying."

I'm thankful for Elliott. He may have just figured a way to beat the system.

❧

15

It's the Least I Can Do

"Among the best home furnishings are children."

— Author Unknown

"**C**ome on, Gampy. You can do it!"

And with those few words from my four-year old grandson Caleb, I climbed up into the fort and prepared to slide, headfirst, down the six-foot slide.

What in the world had brought me to this point?

Well, perhaps it was my Mom who always pitched in and played with us kids.

She hadn't had much of a childhood and I often wondered if it wasn't God's way of showing her a little of the joy of childhood.

She learned the new dances with us, chaperoned at the junior high parties, and helped us make snow ice-cream after we'd all completed the snowman made of some Texas snow. It always contained plenty of dirt and grass that got picked up in the process.

Texas snowmen are *never* pure white, you know.

And it was Momma who insisted that the budget could stand for us to go to the State Fair.

"Kids need that experience," she'd say.

Of course, she'd never had it, but by gosh, we kids were going to.

So when the 4-H bus pulled out, heading for Big D, we kids were on it.

And I never forgot it.

Or maybe it was my Dad who had brought me to this point.

I remember how sister Shirley and I nearly destroyed the family car by learning to drive that old '49 Ford with the stick shift.

Dad had the patience of Job, and when that grinding sound would belch from somewhere under that hood, Dad would softly say, "Remember to push in that left pedal before you shift. You've just about got it!"

And he would participate in other ways, too.

I remember I loved the song, "*Three Coins in the Fountain,*" and we would sit around the table waiting for it to come on the radio. And when it would, it would be my responsibility to write down the first line, and Dad to write down the second line, and Mom to write down the next, and so on.

That plan never worked, but we'd get so tickled trying to figure out who was writing what as the song kept playing and not waiting on any of us.

And I never forgot it.

Or maybe I feel the urge to play with those grandkids because of Miss Yell, my fourth grade teacher who never took a break and actually seemed to look forward to recess as much as we did.

She'd throw the baseball, or push the swings, or get us organized in Red Rover.

And, of course, it was always the first order of business: "Red Rover, Red Rover, let Miss Yell come over."

And here she'd come! Long skirt, clunky heels, and all!

And I never forgot it.

Or maybe I'm doing it because of Aunt Erma, who'd show us kids how to milk a cow and who would get so amused at our efforts.

Or perhaps it was Aunt Minnie who showed us the beauty of planting flowers when we'd visit her for a week during the summer.

Or Aunt Bertha who would get out her oil paints and let us dabble and create all afternoon long on the front porch of her home.

Or could it be Mrs. Huff, my sixth grade teacher, who let me care for her tropical fish in her sunroom after school. She loved things of beauty: great music, fine art, and good books. And she shared them all.

The list of those who went "above and beyond" is endless.

And I never forgot any of them.

So today, as I slide down the slide headfirst, silently praying that the hairpiece stays on, I'm thinking: "Yep, it's payback time."

So, to Caleb, and Taylor, and Hayley, and Dustin, and Annie Francis, and Luke and Anna Rose, and all the other kids in my life: when we're in the middle of the floor playing checkers, or when I'm holding you as you steer the tractor mower, or when I'm reading you a story, or when we're planting a flat of petunias, or when I'm sliding down headfirst, I'm doing it for at least two reasons.

I'm doing it 1) because I love each of you so incredibly much, and 2), because I want to try to emulate those who gave me so much when I was a child.

It's the least I can do.

And kids, I hope you *never* forget it.

16

Puppies: There's Always Space for One More

"Life is the first gift, love is the second, and understanding is the third."

—Author Unknown

E very kid ought to have a dog at least once in his life. Oh, of course they're a lot of trouble. Of course they're expensive. Of course they can complicate your life. (By the way, I'm talking about dogs, not kids; although I can see why you might be confused.)

Our son Todd always wanted pets. We nearly always had a dog when the kids were growing up. Todd had rabbits at one time. We've done the guinea pig thing.

But one dog in particular *always* comes to mind. Her name was "Buttons," and she was the hairiest dog I've ever seen.

It was not her long hair, however, that was her dominant characteristic. Unfortunately, it was her ability to "reproduce."

That's right. Have puppies.

This young lady must have been known all over north Texas, for try as we may, I couldn't keep the "boys" away. And, as you might expect, every few months we'd have another litter.

And because the puppies were so adorable, we nearly always had a waiting list of folks anxious to have one of Button's babies.

The kids of course loved it when there were new puppies. They loved playing with them. They loved watching them eat. It was difficult to leave them alone.

Todd was around three years old at the time one litter was born. And he was so fascinated by the puppies. We talked to him constantly about leaving them with their mother as much as possible, but little boys and puppy dogs just seem to be drawn to one another.

One morning around 6:00 a.m., we awoke to the sound of our five-year old daughter Le'Ann screaming, "Daddy, daddy, come quick! All the puppies are missing!"

Within minutes, Todd proudly announced, "Daddy, I play with de puppies and I put 'em up."

"Where are the puppies?" I asked.

"Lots of places," he proudly announced.

"Todd, can you show Daddy where you put the puppies?"

He immediately went to his bedroom, where he pulled the covers back and exposed one puppy nestled at the foot of his bed.

"Der he is, Daddy," he beamed.

"But where are the others, Todd?" I asked.

His face scrunched up. The eyes looked up to the ceiling, as if he were deep in thought.

"I don't 'member where I put de udders," he muttered after thinking for several minutes.

"Now, Todd, think! We need to find all of the puppies. They need to be with their mother."

Suddenly, as if a light bulb went off, his eyes got wide, a big grin broke out on his face, and he dashed off to the bathroom.

There, huddling up in the bathtub was puppy #2.

Well, this story could run a great deal longer, but to summarize, Todd and I spent the better part of the next hour locating the remaining puppies.

Slowly, almost methodically, the scene would repeat itself. I would ask him to find another puppy. He would ponder, and scrunch, and mutter "I can't 'member where I put de puppies," but then, after a few minutes, the light bulb would go off again.

One puppy was found in the toy box amidst a collection of wooden blocks, pull toys, and stuffed animals. Another was found under his bed. Still another was found in the closet in a shoebox.

Finally, we were down to only one more missing puppy. Todd fretted and wailed and thought and pondered and scrunched some more.

"I can't 'member, Daddy. I can't 'member where de puppy is," he wailed.

"Please, Todd, just think. Calm down and try to remember where you put the other puppy," I pleaded.

All of a sudden, the light went off. The face lit up. The eyes got as big as saucers. The smile stretched from ear to ear.

"I 'member, Daddy! I 'member!" Todd shouted.

And with that, he ran to the den. He grabbed a barstool and started dragging it to the kitchen. He headed straight for the refrigerator. He climbed up on the stool, swung open the refrigerator door, and there, on the top shelf between the milk and the juice, sat a shivering, precious little puppy.

"I find de puppy!" he proudly stated.

Six delightful hiding places. Six slightly shaken puppies. One loving little boy who required constant surveillance. Put it all together, and you have another day, another memory, another delightful story that becomes more precious with time.

17

One of these days I'll laugh about this . . . and today's the day!

"Before I got married, I had six theories about bringing up children.

Now I have six children, and no theories."

—John Wilmot, Earl of Rochester

As I travel around the country talking to school employees, it has become more and more evident how many people can relate to our son, Todd.

The "Todd stories" have become a regular staple of my presentations. I cannot begin to tell you how many hundreds of people have come up to me after one of my talks and said, "I have a Todd. But his name (or her name) is such-and-such."

The similarities are amazing! Like Todd, many of their children had difficulty learning to read. The majority of them didn't "play the school game" well. Most discovered only at the last minute that they were going to graduate. Surprisingly, a large number of them joined the military after high school.

You also need to learn that most of them eventually turned out just fine.

Todd's primary grades were filled with notes from teachers indicating that his progress was slow.

"He's hyperactive," some would tell us.

"He's very social," we often heard.

"Todd is a very interesting child."

His first grade teacher once brought one of Todd's papers to the office. She had a smile across her face and appeared to be holding back the laughter as she gave me some background information.

"We've been doing a creative writing assignment this morning," she began. "I provided a starter sentence and the children's job was to finish it.

"Today's starter sentence was 'I like to read about…'

"The other children wrote that they like to read about dinosaurs, animals, sports and other typical children's books.

"But Todd's answer is unique. In all my years of teaching I've never seen this one," she added.

As she handed me the paper, I was almost afraid to look. Was this about to embarrass me beyond my wildest dreams?

As I read the first sentence of Todd's composition, I understood her laughter.

"I like to read about… *haf a pag.*"

Half a page? How honest can this kid get?

He went on to *explain* how reading is "*a lot of wurk*" and it wore him out. "*I'd ruther be out playin.*"

Oh, it wasn't always easy being the parent of a child like Todd. But, oh, have our efforts paid off!

First of all, we learned so much about children, about love, about life, about living.

We learned that no two children are the same, and that we need to accept those differences and love them for who they are.

We discovered that every child has a gift, and as parents and teachers, we need to nourish, foster, and encourage that special talent.

We realized that patience is a valuable trait for any parent, and that the "fruits of our labors" may not be evident for years.

I'm not going to tell you that we didn't worry and express concern about his schoolwork. I'm not going to say that we did everything right. I'm certainly not going to offer a sure-fire method that works for every child who has some difficulties in school.

But I will "go to the stake," as one of my friends always says, to defend certain ideas and principles that I know will work.

We must always let children know that we love them.

As parents and teachers, we must set standards and limits for our children. And we must remember to model those standards and limits in everything *we* do. As someone wisely said, "we must stand for something, or we will fall for anything."

We must not overreact when our children make mistakes. They're going to make some, just as we did when we were their age.

I believe we must set limits for children. I believe they want us to do just that. As children, many of them are not capable of setting such limits on their own, and they need our guidance and support in order to avoid certain pitfalls along the way.

You've heard it before, but its importance cannot be overemphasized: communicate with your children. Listen intently. Encourage open and honest communication as soon as they're able to talk. Turn off the TV, lay down the paper, and give them your undivided attention.

And finally, give them your time. Giving children your time speaks volumes about how much you care about them. Studies often show that the "average" parent spends only a few moments of quality time each day. How tragic! I'm convinced that the television, the telephone, and casual acquaintances often receive more time and attention than our own children do. I've said it so many times before: "Children spell love, T-I-M-E."

This list is certainly not all-inclusive. All of this and so much more goes into being a good parent.

But in nearly every case, if you'll let your children know you love them... if you'll strive to be a good role model... and if you'll pray for them on a regular basis, one of these days you'll look back, and you'll smile, and you'll realize that your child has turned out all right.

And yes, you'll probably even laugh about some of those difficult days.

If not a laugh, I hope that at least a smile will cross your face as the realization hits you that you weren't such a bad parent.

Why, look how good that kid turned out!

18

A Tribute to Seventeen of the World's Greatest Teachers

"I have always felt that the true textbook for the pupil is his teacher."

— Mohandas K. Gandhi

"Y ou've been influenced by scores of people, maybe even hundreds," the presenter said. "You are the product of each of them."

H-m-m-m-m-m. Really? Well, let me think about that. I know, without a doubt, that teachers had an extraordinary influence on me.

Of course, my first and most important teachers were my parents. And there's no question about their incredible impact.

Mom has always had a remarkable sense of humor. So, when I *do* see the lighter side of what some consider to be extremely serious issues, I thank you, Mom!

From Dad I learned that that a gentle hand and a tender spirit can be powerful forces. And that's *not* a contradiction. So when I get emotional over a hurting child, or I feel an overwhelming need to give someone a much-needed hug, I thank my Dad for providing that.

And what about all those other teachers?

First grade was Mrs. Salmon in Elkart, Texas. She gave me the joy of reading. Thank you, Mrs. Salmon! I use your gift *every* day of my life.

Second grade: Miss Ida Winkle in Mason, Texas. I'll never forget her kneeling beside me during an art assignment and encouraging me to be creative. I suppose that's why I always try to look at things from a different angle to see if there's another way to do them. H-m-m-m-m-m. Maybe so.

By third grade, we were in Brownwood, Texas. And it was Mrs. Hallum who did such a great job with handwriting and math.

Fourth grade introduced me to Miss Yell, who *never* yelled, but who made geography come alive! We'd sail down the imaginary Nile River and "see" all sorts of incredible sights. Thank you for piquing my curiosity about other people and the way they live.

Fifth grade found me in Mrs. Bullion's room. She was a much older teacher, but so much wiser! She taught me multiplication facts, Texas history, and the importance of values.

The second half of that year we moved across town... and I finished the year with Mrs. Bevill. We called her "Bevill the Devil" but she certainly wasn't! She spent all of her extra money on a puppet stage for us and we made puppets and learned the importance of working together. That's likely where I get a flair for drama when I'm presenting. Amazing!

Sixth grade was Mrs. Huff, a master teacher and a major influence. I could write a book about her and the influence she had on me. She incorporated music, art, great literature, and creativity into the lessons, and found time to encourage, listen, laugh, and love every one of us!

My life was changed forever because of her.

Seventh grade was Mr. Lowe, who made science and current events come alive. I learned how important it is to read a newspaper every day.

Eighth grade introduced me to several teachers, but one of the most notable was Mrs. Moore, who left no doubt that she was a Democrat. Suddenly, it made sense to learn about political figures and to vote and to study the issues. Thank you, Mrs. Moore! I think of you every time I cast my ballot.

One of my most impressive ninth grade teachers was Mrs. Doss, the English teacher who said, "Of course you can write! It's inside you! Put it on paper!"

And high school introduced me to Coach Snodgrass, and Mr. Wilson and Mrs. Hurt who each added to the person, *and* the personality, of "yours truly."

And it was Mrs. O'Brien who taught me typing and journalism. And it was also Mrs. O'Brien who encouraged me to be editor of the yearbook. What an experience! What an opportunity!

And it was Miss MacIntosh, the choir teacher, who said, "Of course you can perform in front of people. It takes practice... and you can do it! Trust me. You'll get over the fear of being in front of people."

And, of course, she was right.

There were so many others too numerous to mention.

But, each one worked on me as an individual. Each one chiseled, and hammered, and shaped, and molded and honed me into the person I am today. They not only worked on the head, but they worked on the heart. They influenced not only the actions, but also the attitude.

They not only gave me direction; they gave me their dedication.

And how do I repay them? Interestingly enough, not a one of them expected anything from me in return for their services except to pass it on.

But I think that I am obligated.

I'm obligated not only to them... but to my children, and grandchildren, and nieces and nephews, and my students, and any other young person who comes my way.

What a responsibility! What an obligation! What a debt to try to repay! But what a privilege!

So, to these seventeen, and to the scores who aren't listed, I want to pause for a moment and say "Thank you!" Thank you for giving me a part of yourself. Thank you for doing more than you had to do. Thank you for so masterfully teaching me the lessons of life. Thank you for teaching me so much more than was in the textbook. Thank you for sharing your "gift" with me.

It has truly made all the difference!

19

Confessions of an 11-Year Old Boy on the First Day of School

❧

*"Feel the dignity of a child. Do not feel superior to him,
for you are not."*
-- Robert Henri

When I was a child, I could never go to sleep the night before the first day of school. It was somewhat like the night before Christmas, only this always had an element of fear in it. And the questions kept running through my head as I pondered that first day.

"Will I get a nice teacher?" "Will my friends be in my class?" "Will this grade be so hard I can't pass?"

With those memories in mind, I give you the following fictional account of one such day in the life of one such child.

Yes, it really is fiction. But I have a strong suspicion that at one time or another, it could have been any one of us.

Enjoy. And then, if you work with children, make every effort to be the one who can relieve those fears.

✿

"Where did the summer go?"

I ask myself this question silently as I lay in bed, staring at the ceiling. Tomorrow is the first day of school and I'll finally be a sixth grader. Thought I'd never get here, but all of a sudden, it's time.

As I toss and turn, I can't help but remember last year. I'd never had a teacher like her. She seemed so unhappy. I'm not even sure she liked kids. I know one thing for certain: she didn't like me. I'm not sure she ever knew that it was just my Dad and me. My mom had died when I was very young, and Dad did the very best he knew how. Because he worked at the feed mill, his day started early, and lasted late. He came for one parent conference, but she used such big words, Dad didn't understand most of what she said. He said he probably wouldn't ever do that again.

I remembered the first day of school last year. I had gotten up early, and as I came into the kitchen, Dad said, "Glad to see you wantin' an education, Son. Best thing in the world. An education makes all the difference."

Little did I know how many times I would hear those words from him in the years ahead.

When I arrived at school that morning, I headed straight for the front door where the class rolls were posted.

Once I located my name, I headed down the intermediate hall. I could see a teacher standing in front of my classroom door with her arms crossed.

I remember that as I walked up to her, she said, "Take a seat. Any seat. We'll put you in alphabetical order once everyone gets here and I check the roll. Don't touch the books that are on the desks. Stay seated and no talking."

All of this before I had a chance to even say, "Hello."

That was it. No "Glad to see you," "What's your name?" or "Kiss my foot."

If she'd only smiled.

I do believe that was the longest day of my life. Her classroom was all business. I began to notice that every rule she discussed that day contained either "No" or "Don't." I thought to myself: "We need to add "No laughter and no fun" to the list.

After a couple of hours of her rules, I slowly raised my hand.

"Question?" she asked.

"No, Ma'am. I was just wonderin' if we could have a few "do" rules to go along with all those "do nots."

Everyone laughed... except Teacher.

I shouldn't say I didn't learn anything last year. Actually, I learned a lot.

I learned quickly not to ask questions or contribute anything during class. I learned that days go by much slower when you do nothing but worksheets. I learned that you could think about other things while looking someone right in the eye. I learned that turning in your homework paper is more important than learning anything from it.

I also learned that all teachers are not created equal.

And now, tonight, as I lie in bed wondering what tomorrow holds, I find myself saying a little prayer.

"God, I don't ask for much. But, please, give me a teacher tomorrow who likes me. Let her be someone who likes kids and who makes school fun once in a while. And if she wants to give me an occasional hug or a pat on the back, I wouldn't mind that either. And, Lord, give her a nice smile."

Sometime shortly after that, I fell asleep... and it seemed like only minutes until I heard the alarm ringing beside my bed.

The bus was right on time, and as soon as I stepped off the bus, I hurried to the front door to find my name.

There it was: Room #28, Miss McIver.

She had to be new, as I knew all of last year's sixth grade teacher's names by heart.

I started down the hall. Same strange knot in my stomach. Same fast heartbeat I had every first day of school for as long as I could remember.

As I passed last year's fifth grade classroom, I noticed a new face there, too. What a smile *she* had! Lucky kids.

Room #25... #26...

The pounding had started in my head. I felt my hands begin to tremble a bit. The heart was beating faster than ever.

There she was! Straight ahead! And as I came into earshot of Room #28, I heard the sound of laughter coming from the teacher as she put her arm around the student ahead of me and ushered him into her room.

As she turned back around, she said, "Hi, there! I'm Miss McIver, but you can call me "Miss Mac" if you'd like. Now, tell me your name and I'll do my best to remember it."

I felt her arm around my shoulder. I looked up and saw the biggest smile I'd ever seen.

I smiled back and responded with a choked little "Sure!"

"Make yourself at home," she said. "This is your room, too, you know."

As she rushed to greet the next child, I sat down at the nearest desk.

I simply closed my eyes and quietly whispered, "Thank you, Lord."

20

Gampy, Caleb & Manuel: A Kindergarten Fieldtrip to the Zoo

❧

"I think, at a child's birth, if a mother could ask a fairy godmother to endow it with the most useful gift, that gift should be curiosity."

— *Eleanor Roosevelt*

W e've all seen the book, *All I Really Need to Know I Learned in Kindergarten.*

Well, I tested Fulghum's theory a while back… and it's true.

RaRa and Gampy (as Karen and I are affectionately known to our grandchildren) spent four glorious days caring for them while our daughter and her husband were out of town.

It was during this four-day "re-learning" experience, that I learned of the annual kindergarten field trip to the Fort Worth Zoo.

"Hey! Why not go along in place of the parent?" I asked myself.

So, on a beautiful, early-fall day, I joined a rather large group of very young mothers as chaperones.

"H-m-m-m-m-m. Wonder why they're all whispering, looking at me, and then giggling?" I wondered. "Surely they don't think for one minute that I'm too old to handle this."

If you ask me, some of them looked so young I thought *they* might need a chaperone!

When we arrived at the zoo, I've never seen a more exuberant, excited, invigorated group. Since we arrived a few minutes before the zoo was to open, the children had several minutes to run, ask questions, turn cartwheels, shimmy up poles, climb on railings, hide under benches, crawl on the ground, swing from low-hanging tree limbs, and risk breaking every bone in their bodies.

It was at this moment that I realized why we are often heard to say, "Man, it was a *zoo!*"

I was given temporary custody of my grandson Caleb and a cute little guy named Manuel.

Manuel spoke very little English. He didn't know his last name. But he was a master at running and climbing.

About the only statement I heard him make all day was, "I'm a monkey."

Before the day was over, I understood *exactly* why he thought he was a monkey.

Our first stop at the gorilla and orangutan display found the two little guys giggling and pointing at the more private backside of some small apes.

"Look at his pink bobo, Gampy! Take a picture of it."

Definition: *bobo. A child's name for a derriere.*

I smiled at several older visitors adjacent to us who were giving me a shocked look. I quietly muttered, "He's not mine. I'm just along as a chaperone."

Needless to say, I learned several things that day.

1) A cookie tastes good at anytime of the day. And the birds will eat anything from your lunch that you don't like.

2) Always know where the closest restroom is located.

3) It relieves stress to act like a child occasionally, if only for a few minutes.

4) Kindergarten teachers are born... not made.

And, one last thing: each parent and small group of children was given a different assignment.

Our assignment, given out as we left the school that morning, was to determine the size of a gorilla.

The teacher, Mrs. Maples, is one of those gifted kindergarten teachers who loves the children, has the patience of Job, and the organization of an executive secretary. But I owe her an apology.

"Mrs. Maples, I'm sorry my grandchild told you after the trip that a gorilla was about *your* size, only his arms were longer. I promise I didn't prompt him... at least not *that* much."

As so many have said before about kindergarten teachers: "I don't know what they pay you... but it isn't enough."

21

When It Comes to Children, Expect the Unexpected

"Teaching kids to count is fine, but teaching them what counts is best."

— Bob Talbert

I sn't working with children truly the greatest joy of teaching? After spending thirty years in education, I can't help but smile when I think of certain youngsters with whom I have worked.

Let me tell you about Ross. Ross was a tall, lanky, fifth grader who just couldn't seem to get it together. But he was gifted in other ways.

Persistence was his gift.

I remember once when he lost his speller. Everyday I would ask if he had found it. And everyday I would learn of another location where he had looked... unsuccessfully.

He had looked under his bed, in his closet, in the family car, under the sofa, in the drawers, and at the neighbor's house. He had looked at church, dug in the younger brother's toy box, and searched his desk at school.

The book was nowhere to be found.

Weeks later, Ross bounced into the classroom like a kid with a new toy, only this time he was holding that speller and he could barely talk fast enough to tell me of his good fortune.

"Where? Where did you find it, Ross?" I asked. " I thought you had looked everywhere."

"I found it in the one place I hadn't looked. It was behind the milk jar in the refrigerator."

And then there was Randy. He didn't blow the top out of the academic scoreboard, but he was always trying.

I'd say creativity was his gift.

We were in the middle of a geography lesson on the mid-western states. In the course of study, I told the students that poultry was one of the main products of Oklahoma.

A puzzled look came over the faces of several students.

"Oh, some of you may not be familiar with the word 'poultry.' Who can give us the definition?"

Several hands went up, but none so exuberantly as Randy's.

"I know! I know! *Please* let me tell," he begged.

Randy rarely knew the answers, and I was pleased that he had this one in the bag.

"OK, Randy. Define 'poultry' for us."

"Poultry is what you call a poem that rhymes," he responded proudly.

And, apparently, it's becoming much more challenging to teach today's youngsters.

A teacher recently shared with me a problem that is becoming all too frequent.

It seems that Joe Bob (and she swears that was his name) was a very vocal and exuberant second grader. During recess, several of the youngsters ran up to the teacher and told her that Joe Bob has said the "D-word."

One child quietly and distinctly whispered: "He said 'damn,' Teacher."

The teacher sent the children back to play, and pulled Joe Bob off to the side.

"The children tell me that you have been using bad language. Would you please tell me what you said?" the teacher asked.

"I don't remember," Joe Bob promptly responded.

"Now think, Joe Bob. What did you say that you shouldn't have?"

"Was it "@&$#!" Joe Bob asked.

"No! No! It certainly wasn't!" the teacher muttered, with her mouth hanging open.

"Well... was it "%$&%@?" he innocently asked?

"Oh, no! It wasn't that either," the teacher responded, gasping for breath.

In desperation, Joe Bob looked her right in the eye and said, "Well... if you'll give me the beginning letter, I'll try to figure it out!"

His gift? A remarkable vocabulary for a second grader.

Spend some time with a child today. It's one of the ways an adult learns.

22

Kids: They Call It like They See It

*"Loving a child is a circular business . . .
the more you give, the more you get,
the more you get, the more you give."*

— Penelope Leach

Oh, he was a pretty typical little guy from any elementary school, anywhere.

Second grade, full of life, BIG smile, and more charisma than any politician who ever lived.

He had that charm and honesty that you couldn't miss. And, once he had said his piece, and had started his half-run, half-walk back to class, you would always smile, chuckle a bit, shake your head, and be thankful he had crossed your path another day.

By the end of the first day of school you knew him. As the new principal of the new school, he was one of those you would tell your family about during the evening meal.

He had bounced out of nowhere, and said, "Hi! Are you the principal?"

"Sure am," I said. "My name is Mr. Jordan."

Before I could utter another sound, he reported his observations to me.

"Gosh you're tall... and you sure do have a big mouth! My name is Sean and my mom says that that's not your real hair. Is it?"

"Sure it's mine," I stammered. Then I gave him a huge smile and a pat on the back and said, "If you pay good money for something, it's yours, isn't it?"

"Yeah," he responded.

And that was the end of that.

I also remember the first time he came to my office. He was sent there for "misbehaving." I gave him my usual "You can do so much better than this" talk, and I could tell from his silence that he was doing a lot of thinking. When we were finished, he stood up, looked at me with those big dark eyes and said, "I'll tell you one thing, Mr. Jordan. Starting today, I'm going to turn my life around! And I mean it!"

H-m-m-m-m. Some days go better than others.

As the year progressed, he and I became great friends. He would stop me in the hall and share all sorts of information. I nearly always heard how he had spent his weekend. I always found out when some other student had done something inappropriate that *he* had witnessed. And I always heard about the little league games that he played.

When Christmas came around, he shared his love for his teacher in a new and profound way. As he laid a rather crudely wrapped package on her desk, he proudly announced: "I love you so much, Teacher, that I decided to *waste* some money on you... and buy you a present."

That line must have been repeated in the lounge a dozen or more times that day!

And, on the last day I would serve as school principal prior to "retiring," he would once again leave me with a treasured gem.

Amongst all the notes and cards and gifts was one crudely written message which simply said: "Mr. Jordan, Thak you for all you hav done for me. I will nevr forgat you. You are the *beast* princible in the world." Love, Your friend, Sean."

Surely... surely... he meant "best."

But, as we have to be reminded from time to time: kids generally call it like they see it!

❧

23

The Smells of Summer vs. the Smells of 'Back-to-School'

"First things first! But not necessarily in that order."

—Author Unknown

I'm pretty sure that scientists are seriously involved in a study to determine why summer is the shortest season of the year. There's no way that an average school day is as short as one of the days when the kids are out for the summer.

In spite of this quirk of nature, the signs are everywhere that *(read this in a whisper)* "the start of school is just around the corner."

The first indication I had that it wouldn't be long until the start of school was when I was in my favorite shopping spot: Wal-Mart. I headed for the garden section, and what to my wandering eyes should appear, but boxes and boxes of school supplies being unpacked and placed on the shelves!

The latest Disney lunch boxes, along with the familiar aroma of crayons and scented markers had replaced the smell of potting soil and Sevin dust!

Now, don't get me wrong. I love that smell. I've always loved the smell of new school supplies. In fact, one of the saddest days of all was when they quit selling that wonderful white paste. Gosh, I loved the smell of that! I'll never forget Charlie Thompson across the aisle from me in Mrs. Hallum's third grade classroom. He ate it in huge chunks. I don't think it hurt him. It was probably made out of wheat or some other grain, and I suspect that he thought it looked like a really bad bowl of cereal.

Anyway, he'd go through a bowl of it, or rather a jar, once or twice a week. And he *was* the biggest kid in third grade!

A lot of the supplies I bought as a child aren't on the shelves anymore.

When did mucilage disappear? And what about those wonderful Mongol colored pencils? And do you remember ink eradicator? Now *there* was an aroma!

Of all the smells I remember, nothing could compare to freshly run purple ditto sheets. No wonder kids of the sixties were so different. They'd been sniffing freshly run purple ditto sheets for years!

Add to that the smell of pencil shavings, the just-swept, oily wooden floors, and a still-wet blackboard, and you are back to the classroom I remember as a child.

So, if you have a few days of "vacation" left before the start of school, savor those memorable smells of summer.

Breathe deeply when the grass is being mowed. U-h-m-m-m-m-m-m.

Open that bottle of coconut flavored suntan lotion, and rub a bit on the back of your hand. U-h-m-m-m-m-m-m!

Stop by the snow cone stand and order your favorite. The strawberry is hard to beat. Yeah!

Bite into a fresh, tree-ripened peach. If the juice runs down your cheek, you're doing it right. H-u-m-m-m-m-m-m!

Dig down into a bag of potting soil, and smell that rich, moist humus. U-h-m-m-m-m-m-m.

And this weekend, make one last freezer-full of fresh homemade vanilla ice cream.

Y-e-o-w-w-w-w-w!

Now you're talking!

A-h-h-h-h-h. The smells of summer. A-h-h-h-h-h. The smells of back-to-school.

Enjoy the moment.

"To every thing there is a season, and a time to every purpose under the heaven." Ecclesiastes 3:1

24

Maybe Tomorrow
Will Be Better

❧

"Challenge can be stepping stones or stumbling blocks. It's just a matter of how you view them."
—Author Unknown

If you've been in public education for any length of time at all, you begin to notice how many things have changed.

Now, don't get me wrong. I love change. I always have. There's something new and exciting and stimulating about change.

It gets you out of the humdrum routine you're in and allows you to be excited about tomorrow.

Someone was quoted as saying not *too* long ago that if someone who had died fifty years ago were brought back to life, the only thing he'd recognize would be the public schools.

Sorry... but I disagree.

I started thinking about all the things that have changed since I first entered a classroom just over thirty years ago.

There were 38 children in my fifth grade classroom before that year ended. But, that was so much better than the 50 students that Mrs. Bledsoe had when I did my student teaching.

There was no carpet on the floors and no air conditioning. The PTA project that year was to buy a box fan for every room.

Student worksheets were run on the one spirit duplicator in the office. The purple copies, more often than not, were barely readable.

Of course we didn't have computers, or television sets, or video tape players. We *did* have a 16-millimeter film projector in the building, but the films were usually antiquated, and frequently, not on grade level.

We got our news from *The Weekly Reader.* Gotta tell you though, I enjoyed that interesting little publication.

The first order of business was to try to get all the lunch money collected before the morning announcements, pledge, and prayer were made over the intercom. Yeah. A prayer! A different student prayed every morning.

Our library consisted of a truck, which delivered books once a week that the children had ordered from an out-dated list of titles.

Teachers ate lunch with their children, took them to PE, exercised with them, laughed with them, played ball with them.

We taught the art and the music and did the counseling.

We helped check their eyesight, their hearing, their height, and their weight.

I could go on and on, but you get the picture.

However, there are some things that *never* seem to change.

Last week, a sad little girl in my neighborhood was walking home from school. As I was working in the front yard, she stopped to visit.

"How was school today?" I asked.

"Not so good. A bunch of girls in my room made fun of me." Her long, unkempt hair circled those sad, dark eyes.

"I'm so sorry," I said. "Try to think about something else. Try to think about something good that happened today."

Here was a child who was being raised by a father who worked long hours. There was no mother in her life. There was no one to prepare her balanced meals. There was no one to show her how to fix her hair. There was no one to match her clothes. There was no role model to teach her about being a lady.

Cruel, hurting, remarks are still with us after all these years.

As she walked away, I remembered my childhood. I remembered joining in when someone would make a cruel statement about a deprived, homely little girl in our classroom. Her name was Drucy. The very name lent itself to ridicule.

"I don't want to sit by Drucy! I'll get germs!"

"Teacher, Drucy smells bad."

"Drucy... you look like a goosey!"

Drucy would look at us as if we'd stabbed her again. She had stopped retaliating. She had stopped fighting back.

And then one day as we were being dismissed from school, I heard the sound of an ambulance getting closer to the school. I saw a crowd of people gathering at the intersection.

And as I got closer, her name was being echoed from all directions.

"Drucy! It's Drucy! She's been hit by a car! They say she won't survive. Can you believe it? Drucy! Drucy Goosey!"

I never had an opportunity to tell her how sorry I was I had not defended her. But I've never forgotten her.

We now have amazing technology, support services, smaller classes, improved libraries, extra-curricular activities, beautiful buildings, and on and on and on.

And one day I'd love to be able to say: "Oh, yeah, and there's another thing that's changed: people no longer say hurtful things to one another.

As my sad, little lonely neighbor walked on down the street, I yelled, "I'm sorry, Sweetie. I sure hope tomorrow's better."

And then I looked heaven-ward, and closed my eyes, and whispered, "I'm sorry, Drucy. I know things are better for you now."

❧

Laugh Your Way to Better Health and a Trimmer Waistline

"Laughing at our mistakes can lengthen our life.

Laughing at someone else's can shorten it."

—Author Unknown

OK. It's time we take something seriously.

I'm talking laughter.

Hey... it's pretty serious stuff.

Did you know that researchers have now determined that when you laugh, all sorts of things happen internally? Some call it "inner jogging." Apparently, everything gets jostled around. You give it all a good workout.

And you never have to leave the comfort of your easy chair.

Laughing, researchers tell us, is "hearty medicine" that boosts the immune system and triggers a "flood of pleasure-inducing neurochemicals" in the brain.

I think we all need more pleasure-inducing neurochemicals without having to take a pill to get them. This sounds like a good plan.

In addition, we now know that when you let out one of those really good gut-wrenching laughs, your body burns calories. Researchers have sat around the laboratory, laughing like crazy, while someone counted all those little calories as they were consumed during this experiment.

And guess what they discovered.

You burn 78 times as many calories while laughing as when you are in a resting state.

Some of us even laugh during the resting state.

Recently, I woke up in the middle of the night hearing my wife singing *"O Come, All Ye Faithful."* Here she was, sound asleep, singing as coherently as she could with a pillow covering half her face.

I couldn't resist. I accepted her invitation as joyfully and triumphantly as I could. I started singing harmony.

And it wasn't bad. I think it was the closest I came to getting the Christmas spirit this year.

When I got a little too loud on the final strains, she woke up, and wanted to know what in the world I was doing?

Her comments were not exactly in the Christmas spirit.

And then we started laughing, and I told her how much weight we were losing. With that comment, she lost her sense of humor and went back to sleep.

When you laugh, researchers tell us that our heart and lungs are stimulated. You breathe deeper and therefore, oxygenate more blood.

The most important finding, however, is that your body releases endorphins when you laugh. Those are the natural "painkillers." They are the ones that destroy viruses and tumors. A disease-fighting protein, gamma-interferon, rises with laughter, as well as B-cells. They produce more disease-destroying antibodies.

So... why aren't we laughing more?

But now, one of the most interesting statistics I've ever read. Did you know that children, on average, laugh about 400 times a day! That averages out to about a chuckle, or chortle, or giggle, or hoot about every two minutes kids are awake.

But there's another tragic part to this statistic: adults typically only laugh about 15 times a day. That averages out to less that one an hour on a typical day.

Why do we adults lose 385 laughs a day?

Good question. Obviously, we take this business of life too seriously.

So, if you want to lose weight, be healthier, happier, and live longer, I suggest you laugh more. Laugh a lot. Laugh loud.

As my hero Will Rogers once said, "We are all here for a spell. Get all the good laughs you can."

And my favorite animator, Charles Schultz, puts it this way, "If I were given the opportunity to present a gift to the next generation, it would be the ability for each individual to learn to laugh at himself."

Till next time... keep laughing!

It's certainly my weight-loss plan.

"I Knew That!"

❀

"Never argue with a stupid person. First, they'll drag you down to their level, then they will beat you with experience."

—Author Unknown

W hoever said that we learn from our mistakes was really on to something.

In spite of the learning that takes place, sometimes it can certainly make you feel stupid.

As many of you know, my wife and I moved, following "retirement," from the "big city" to the "little town." We moved from the Dallas-Fort Worth area to a beautiful, quaint little town called Hamilton, Texas.

But being a "city boy" in the country can make you feel awfully stupid.

Recently, I found myself standing around with several men, women and children admiring a field of livestock.

"That's quite a gelding over there, isn't it?" one of the men commented as he pointed at this beautiful animal.

Everyone agreed.

And before I knew it, I heard myself saying:

"Geldings. They look an awful lot like horses, don't they?"

That moment of silence when everyone is thinking, "Did he say what I think he said," seemed like hours.

Finally, I heard a child's voice saying, "A gelding is a horse. It means that he's been..."

But before the eight-year old could finish, his mother slapped her hand over his mouth.

"I was just kidding," I lied as I slapped my knee.

Everyone laughed... except my wife, who knew better.

It's a whole different world here in central Texas.

However, making such remarks at inappropriate times is not limited to just being here in Hamilton, Texas.

When I first started teaching I was in the lounge one day and several teachers were being critical of the school board members for not giving a bigger salary increase.

After listening for a while, I commented, "And no telling how much of a salary they make being on that board!"

Duh.

Again, I learned something.

George Bernard Shaw's quote makes me feel better.

"A life spent in making mistakes is not only more honorable but more useful than a life spent in doing nothing."

But before I start feeling too good about all the mistakes I make, I'm reminded of another quote: "To err is human, but when the eraser wears out ahead of the pencil, you're overdoing it."

27

"Who Ya Gonna Blame?"
It's a Good Question!

❧

"Sometimes I lie awake at night and I ask 'Where have I gone wrong?'

Then a voice says to me, 'This is going to take more than one night.'"

—Charlie Brown

O K. I'm not blaming my parents for any mistakes I make as an adult. My behavior can't be blamed on any of my teachers. Other adults and relatives helped a great deal in my "upbringing," and I give them nothing but praise as well.

But, dad-gum-it. You *gotta* blame somebody.

And in my case, it was my sister.

It's like a recurring nightmare. It happens every time I'm in a Toys-R-Us, or ride a bicycle, or see a parade. Yep, she's the reason!

It all happened with I was in the fifth grade and she was in the third. It actually began that Christmas, when we got one bicycle to share.

"Santa could only afford *one*," Mom and Dad tried to explain.

Now for a boy to ride a girl's bicycle is bad enough, but in my neighborhood it was inhumane! It was the kiss of death!

I would ride that bike late at night, when the sun went down and the kids went in. I would sail down those semi-darkened streets in my neighborhood and consider it the best fifteen minutes of the day.

Then summer came to central Texas. Those were hot, muggy, long days as we neared the Fourth of July celebration.

The local radio station and newspaper began promoting the children's bike parade. Prizes were to be awarded to the top three best-decorated bicycles.

Well, obviously, I couldn't ride in it... but I could pour every nickel and dime I had from my downtown newspaper sales into crepe paper and flags.

And so, on that hot summer morning, I blew every cent I had on red, white, and blue decorations. I taped, and wrapped, and studied and planned, while sister just watched. Mom dressed her in red, white, and blue and the race was on!

In spite of scores of entries, it was announced following the parade that sister (and I, of course) had won second place... and we were to meet in the city park in one hour for the awarding of prizes.

Upon arrival, we found tables on an outdoor stage *laden* with gifts. And there, standing out as if God Himself was shining a beacon of light from Heaven on it, was the one game I had wanted all my life. It was the one my little rich cousin had, and if we were real nice to her when we would go to her home for our summer "vacation," she would let us play with it for a half-hour or so.

Yes, there it was... for the taking... a brand new Cootie game!

"Oh, my gosh, Sister.... LOOK! A Cootie game!" I barely uttered.

"Yeah," she casually muttered.

In-as-much as we were the second place winners, the first place winner got first choice.

"Don't take the Cootie game," I prayed. "Please don't pick up the Cootie game!"

When I opened my eyes, it was still there.

It was my earliest recollection of God answering a prayer... and so *quickly!*

"YES! It's still there!" I yelled.

Then, I found myself singing: "We're going to get a Cootie game.... We're going to get a Cootie game."

Sister slowly walked upon that stage and began casually sauntering around the table, reviewing all the gifts.

"Pick up that Cootie game," I yelled. "We're gonna have a Cootie game." The singing had started up again.

But then, I noticed she was deep in thought. I suddenly realized she was a thousand miles away and she wasn't listening to one word I was screaming.... *or singing!*

Then, without warning, she picked up the one gift that I wouldn't have given you ten cents for: toilet water!

Yep. Toilet water.

I was in shock. I stood staring at that Cootie game with my mouth hanging open as Sister came prancing down the steps with her toilet water.

She was beaming as she announced, "Look, everybody! Toilet water! Like the rich folks use!"

It was the longest ride home of my life!

And, promptly upon arriving at home, Sister proved how knowledgeable she was about life's finer toiletries. Sister did exactly what any unknowing person with a big bottle of toilet water might do. She promptly began sprinkling it ... *in the toilet!*

"It wouldn't say toilet water if you weren't supposed to put it in your toilet!" she insisted.

I never got over it. So when I'm in a toy store, that ray of light comes down and shines on (you guessed it!) ...the Cootie game!

And when I see a parade, I think about the Cootie game!

And when it's the Fourth of July, I think about the Cootie game!

But why am I telling you this story?

Because I recently experienced the best Christmas present ever!

Thanks, Sis, for the Cootie game... even if it did come forty years late.

But you know, no one *ever* had a better smelling bathroom than we did! And for that, I give you *all* the credit!

Love, Brother Riney

The More You Give...
The More You Receive

"*Humans are like tea bags. They never realize their strength until they are put in hot water.*"

—Author Unknown

Everything good in life comes with a price.
I found that out the hard way.

There I am, sitting at my desk, minding my own business, when the call comes in that will change my life for the next several months.

"Riney, I'm a promotional manager for a large candy company, and we're about to introduce a new health bar around the country. I understand that you know a lot of people and that you're always promoting something, right?"

"Uh, yeah, I guess, sorta."

"Well, would you mind if I sent you some free candy bars? They'll come in double chocolate, chocolate-chip, and chocolate peanut butter, and all you have to do is give them away. These delicious bars are called Kudos and we think you and your friends are really going to like them."

"They're, uh, *free*?" I stammered.

"That's right. We're just going to send them to you to distribute to as many people as you can. Now, are there any large special events coming up anytime soon?" the marketer asked.

"Yeah, uh, there's homecoming in two weeks... and it's a big deal. Several thousand folks attend," I added.

"Perfect," she responded. "Could you give me an estimate of how *many* thousand?"

Now I've never been good with numbers. I've noticed that I tend to exaggerate. I suffer from that "bigger's gotta be better" syndrome.

"Uh, probably *twenty* thousand? I know we have to bring in extra bleachers... and the stadium is huge. People sit on the grassy slopes and they're everywhere. Yeah... I'd say about twenty thousand."

"Great!" she said. "Well, since there are three different flavors, we'd like for them to get to try each one of them, so I'll send you enough to give each person there three bars apiece. OK?"

"Sure," I said. "Wonderful!"

And with that, I began working on some other projects, and didn't give it another thought... *until the front receptionist called back to my little office a couple of weeks later.*

"Riney, there's a man here with a delivery for you. He says it's a truck full of candy bars."

"Oh, yeah, that will be the candy we're going to distribute to everyone at the homecoming game. Just tell him to bring the boxes back here to my office."

Silence. Then I hear discussion between the two of them... and then laughter.

"He says his 18-wheeler is packed. We don't think they'll fit in your office," she giggled.

I walked up front to visit with him, and we determined they would have to go to the warehouse. A quick call over there quickly reflected that the warehouse crew wasn't very happy with me, but they'd help me out.

For the next hour and a half, the warehouse crew and I tossed and stacked boxes until we were exhausted. When we finished, I counted 120 huge boxes. I opened one of them and found that each big box contained twenty-four smaller boxes. Each small box contained twenty-four bars. A calculator revealed that I was the trustee of 69,120 candy bars. And in my generosity, I gave each of the guys a couple of the small boxes. They were pleased... and I was down to just slightly over 69,000 bars!

The homecoming parade was scheduled for that afternoon, so I gave each of the four floats a huge box to share with the spectators.

"Just toss them to the folks as you go down Main Street," I instructed.

Obviously, the word "toss" didn't mean the same to me as it did them.

Believe it or not, a chocolate bar with nuts can become a lethal weapon when hurled at top speed by a member of the football team. Little kids were crying as the bars came hurtling through the air. Minor injuries were everywhere that day.

I got hit in the head by one of them. It turned my hairpiece from a north-south direction to an east-west direction in a flash. Actually, I'm convinced that that head of hair kept me from getting a concussion.

Nevertheless, we distributed just over 2300 bars. I only needed to give away 66,000 of them at the game.

Unfortunately, there weren't 20,000 people at the football game, and as hard as I tried, we only gave out about half the bars. The band boosters who ran the concession stands said they had never had a worse night. "We'll be years recovering from this loss" was the last thing I heard as I walked to my car late that evening.

I got a call on Monday from the candy company, anxious to hear how the bars were received.

"Great, just great. Everybody loved them," I reported.

"Did you have any left?" she asked.

"Yeah. Yeah, we had a few left, but I'm going to distribute those at the citywide festival coming up in a couple of weeks. It's a big deal with people coming in from all over the state, and I'll hand out the rest of them there."

"Wonderful! By the way... how many people usually attend the festival?"

"Oh, thousands, probably 50,000. It's a big one!" I responded.

"Tell you what I'm going to do," she said. "To make sure you have enough, I'm going to send you two more truckloads for you to distribute at the festival!"

I was speechless.

Well, to wrap this up, I received somewhere in the neighborhood of 200,000 candy bars. My entire family spent the festival giving away Kudos. We used them at Halloween for trick or treaters, as did virtually every other family in town. I sent one home with every student every Friday for weeks. Every school lounge had a case.

But it's a job to get rid of 200,000 of *anything!*

The local grocer refused to stock them for years, stating simply: "Who'd buy them? Every house in town has a stack of them in their freezer."

This was several years ago now. But when I retired, more than one person gave me a box of Kudos.

And, if you're ever through Hamilton, Texas and want to stop by the house for a few minutes, you'll have your choice of double chocolate, chocolate chip, or chocolate peanut butter Kudos.

But just remember: everything good in life comes with a price.

"Memories of a Special Child"

"Most great men and women are not perfectly rounded in their personalities, but are instead people whose one driving enthusiasm is so great it makes their faults seems insignificant."

—Charles Cerami

O h, we've all had them in our classrooms. You'll find them in schools all around the world. And everywhere they have touched the hearts of those who know them.

These special youngsters come to us in wheelchairs, with metal limbs, with slurred speech. Some come with constant muscle contractions. They often drool. Their needs can be almost constant.

As parents, we've all checked our children at birth for ten fingers and ten toes. But the parents of these special youngsters realize almost immediately that while there probably were ten fingers and ten toes, something was different. And as the days progressed, what they knew in their heart became a reality as the doctor shared the findings.

However, after observing hundreds of these youngsters, I have discovered some amazing facts about our special children and their special parents.

First, I challenge you to find any child who is happier than our special children. When we around them, we have this insatiable desire to hug them and try to return a portion of the love that they radiate.

And I believe that their parents are generally the most patient, caring parents in the world.

God's plan for matching children with appropriate parents cannot be improved upon.

I remember one young boy in particular. His mother brought him to school when he was old enough to enroll in kindergarten. And she made a special effort to introduce him to as many members of the staff as possible.

Scott was such a little charmer! This precious little blonde-headed guy was already overweight, but had the most captivating smile I've ever seen. And although he required a great deal of help, he preferred to do things for himself.

Almost immediately I admired his courage and his drive. A simple task of picking up a pencil was a major job. Keeping the paper still while he attempted to write was a lesson in patience. But Scott was no quitter.

And as the years passed, Scott's list of friends grew. It seemed that everyone knew him and loved him.

He would go to great extremes to call out your name at the grocery store. He would wave frantically when he spotted you driving. And he loved attending local high school football games. He was unquestionably the team's biggest and most loyal fan.

When he began attending middle school, I would often make an extra effort to drop by his classroom to have my spirits lifted. When you're feeling a little down, these special children will always improve your mood.

I recall one day when the teacher was conducting a cooking lesson. Walking Scott through the production of tollhouse cookies would be like walking me through piloting a 747. This was no easy task, but he loved it!

During his high school years, he always brought a date to the annual homecoming game. His special girlfriend would always have a huge corsage, and Scott would be dressed to the hilt. And when the two of them started the walk down the steps to find a seat, it was as if everything stopped. Every eye was on them as if the bride and groom were walking the aisle. And that smile on his face alone could have lit the stadium!

When Scott graduated from high school, he received a standing ovation. Someone explain to me why tears always accompany extreme joy.

Many of us wondered what would happen to Scott after graduation. But when a new Luby's cafeteria opened up a few years later, there was Scott, greeting and cleaning tables. He proudly told me that he was learning to drive and that he had talked his Mom into letting him move into an apartment by himself.

I immediately pictured him making tollhouse cookies and wondering how long cleanup would take.

I talked to him in the cafeteria a couple of years ago. It was the start of the Christmas season and he told me how he'd gone to Wal-Mart, bought Christmas decorations, and had put up his own tree.

"I bought a real good artificial tree so I'll have it every year," he told me. "I love Christmas."

A few months ago, I spotted Scott's photo on the obituary page of the *Ft. Worth Star-Telegram*. There was no explanation of his death.

And as I sat there in utter disbelief, a tear rolled off my cheek and was immediately absorbed by the newsprint.

You probably didn't know him. Some might even think his life was lived in vain. But for those of us who knew Scott, we'll never forget his smile, his gentleness, and his love for all people

And if you want to experience a bit of his charm, spend some time with a special child today.

You'll discover it with their first smile.

And immediately you'll understand why we call them "special."

30

"They Also Teach Who Only Set an Example"

❧

"Respect cannot be learned, purchased, or acquired — it can only be earned.

—Author Unknown

It seemed as if Mark was always in trouble. He rarely completed assignments, his language was foul, and he was constantly caught stealing from the other students. His hair was unkempt, his clothes were dirty, and he had a distinctive odor. He was failing fourth grade... and *we* were failing him.

I was his principal and had visited with Mark on several occasions. But, quite frankly, nothing seemed to be changing as a result of our conversations.

As he sat in front of me once again with his head hanging down and a dejected look on his face, I asked him why he had been sent to the office.

"I stoled some tenny shoes from a kid's locker yesterdy."

I wanted to tell him that a good thief would wait a few days before wearing them back to school, but I knew that wouldn't be appropriate.

After discussing the incident in the usual manner, I casually asked, "Have you stolen anything else here at school?"

I wasn't prepared for the answer... or should I say *answers*?

He spent the next fifteen minutes confessing to every item he had ever stolen at school: crayons, books, money, toys, food, jackets, and toboggans. The list was endless.

After a few minutes of this, I began fumbling for a pencil to make some notes. This kid was one for the record book!

Once he appeared to be at the end, I took a deep breath, realized my mouth was hanging open, shut it, and pondered for a few moments.

"I feel I have to share this with your parents," I told him.

I called his house and his mom answered after several rings. Rather than go into all the details over the phone, I asked her if it would be possible to come to the school to discuss a problem we were having with Mark. She said she'd be there in a few minutes.

As she entered the office, I noticed some similarities: her hair was unkempt, her clothes were dirty, and she had a distinctive odor. *H-m-m-m-m-m.* I also noticed the unmistakable smell of alcohol on her breath.

She gave me a huge hug, looked me right in the eye, and, this is an exact quote, said to me: "What's the problem, Hon?"

Why did I feel that she would call me "Hon" the rest of the meeting?

Mark and I spent the next several minutes repeating the offense. Actually, I should say "*offenses*."

When we finished, I will never forget her comment and her reaction. She stood up, held on to the chair for support, squinted her eyes at Mark and somewhat growled as she said, "I can't believe you stoled anything. You know good and well that your Daddy and I have taught you better'n than that! You're gonna catch it when you git home today, buddy!"

At that point, Mark stood up, and started wailing, "That ain't true, Momma. You know Daddy steals all the time from work… and he sneaks over to the neighbor's house and steals tools from his pickup… and he…."

"Shut up, Mark! Shut up, Mark!" she squealed. "That's a d— lie! He ain't never stoled nothing in his life! Shut up, Mark!"

As they continued to shout at one another with accusations, I realized that once again my mouth was hanging open and my head was jerking from left to right as I would look at the person doing the talking… or should that be screaming?

When it was all over, I walked Mark out into the hall, told him we would talk again, gave him a hug, and suddenly saw him in a whole new light.

As I stepped back into the office, his mom was now sitting. Her head was hanging down and she had a defeated look on her face.

Here was a mother silently wondered why her child was stealing… but secretly knowing why.

And so, day after day, similar stories happen in schools, in homes, in offices, in government.

Some parents allow their teenagers to drink alcohol at home and they silently wonder why children are being killed for driving drunk.

Headlines read about some school board members who cannot conduct a civil meeting because of their poor conduct. And they silently wonder why students are not being respectful.

We see professional athletes cursing, losing control, and being removed from sporting events, and we silently wonder why children do not have self-control.

Entertainers admit to having sexual relationships outside of marriage and America silently wonders why its youth are so sexually active.

Our elected leaders routinely admit they lied to the American public, and we silently wonder why our children do not trust one another.

Unfortunately, the grades are in... and too often, our examples deserve ample "X's"

"When you walk what you talk... people listen."

"Your job gives you authority. Your behavior earns you respect."
–Irwin Federman

"We expect our leaders to be better than we are... and they should be – or why are we following them?" —*Walt Disney*

To paraphrase a Chinese general: If *the world is to be better, my country must first be changed. If my country is to be changed, my community must be improved. If my community is to be improved, my family must be right. If my family is to be right, I myself must be a good example.*

But my all-time favorite comes from Albert Schweitzer. It says it more plainly, more clearly, more direct than any quote about being a good example than anything that I've ever read.

"Example is not the main thing in influencing others. It is the <u>*only*</u> *thing."*

Wow! Do I know some politicians who could use that one!

31

"And It's Only Tuesday"

"We often see further through a tear than through a telescope."

—Author Unknown

The week started like any other.

Monday came. I manage to get up after an exhausting weekend. And I find myself in the usual routine once again.

I work. I put in a full day. I quit around 5:00 o'clock. The wife and I have dinner and relax a bit. We watch the 10:00 o'clock news. We go to bed.

It's now Tuesday morning. Another day.

"Just like yesterday," I say to myself.

I get to the office. I make a few phone calls. The morning drags. I'm tired already.

And it's only Tuesday.

I begin my usual routine. It's just one big déjà vu.

Been there. Done that.

I look at the clock. It's 11:30 a.m. It's almost time for lunch.

Same routine. Same old typical day.

And it's only Tuesday.

But as I'm eating lunch, the wife walks in and says, "There's been another school shooting."

We turn on the television set and I begin to watch a horror unfolding. Children are running from a high school. The reports are sketchy. Bodies everywhere. Bombs. Guns. Chaos.

I numbly watch as parents run toward the school, fearful of what they might find, or not find. I feel myself living the fear with them.

I see fifteen and sixteen-year-old children crying uncontrollably. I see children and parents and teachers embracing and consoling and loving and caring. I see young boys crawling out of windows and falling several feet. They're horrified. They're literally running for their lives. I see more tears than perhaps I've seen in a lifetime.

My thoughts are the same thoughts everyone is having. Why is this happening? Who in their right mind could commit such an atrocity?

Any parent's worst nightmare is being played out with real people, real blood, real loss of life.

As the drama continues to unfold, I find myself praying for those involved. I close my eyes and feel real tears rolling down my cheeks at the thought of my own children having to experience such a horror. I look at the young girls and imagine my own daughters on the screen. I hear stories coming from brave young men and I pray that my own son would have reacted in such a heroic manner.

As the camera rolls and the minutes tick away into hours, I learn of a teacher who lost his life in the shooting. From all accounts, this was no ordinary teacher, but one who exemplified the virtues we all want for our children. He taught not only the subject matter, but more importantly, he taught students how to live.

And today, he taught students how to die.

The network breaks for local news, and I feel a bit guilty for wanting to think about something else for a few minutes.

"Two small children were found today in a creek bottom. They have not been reported missing and their identify is unknown," the commentator reads.

I've been numbed by the news of the shooting, and I briefly feel the pain of losing two more precious children.

"In other Texas news, authorities still have no leads in the disappearance of a young girl who disappeared from her home today...."

My heart has never felt heavier.

"What's happened today?" I want to scream. "Why are our children having to pay the price for a sick society? Leave them alone! Leave them alone! Leave them alone!"

My mind is screaming, but I'm too shocked to make a sound.

I get up. I walk to the phone. I call our children and tell them how much I love them. I want to hear our grandchildren tell me that they love me. This is better than any sedative, better than any medicine.

I hang up the phone and realize that I've been silently weeping through the entire conversation.

Stability. That's what I need. I need a guarantee that life will be good and that my children and my grandchildren and their children will never have to endure such a travesty.

But down deep, I know there are no such guarantees.

I look at the calendar hanging there in the kitchen. Tuesday, April 20, 1999.

Fourteen children and one teacher are dead in Colorado. Two unidentified children are found dead in Central Texas. A young girl has been abducted in North Texas.

As I lie in bed, staring at the ceiling, thinking of the horrors of the day, I realize that children need loving, caring individuals in their lives more than ever. They need to know we're there for them. They need to have us to listen. They need for us to instill strength and courage and wisdom. They need us to be examples of how to live. They need us to be not just their friends, but their role models. They need for us to be involved in their lives. They need so much and we realize that our window of opportunity goes by much too quickly.

Today has changed me forever. And if nothing else, it has confirmed to me that our mission of hope for today's children needs to be shouted louder than ever before. The needs have never been greater. The cry for help has never been more clearly sounded.

My God. All in one day.

And it's only Tuesday.

All the Difference

32

For All of You Who Didn't Win the Education Award

"The ultimate measure of an individual is not where he stands in moments of comfort and convenience, but where he stands at times of challenge and controversy."

—Martin Luther King, Jr.

I recently read an article dedicated to all of those moms who hadn't been named "Mother of the Year." It was for all of those mothers who go about their tasks on a daily basis, who love what they're doing, who often go unappreciated and unnoticed.

This same premise is true for educators as well. So, with that in mind, I dedicate this to all of you who haven't been named "Educator of the Decade."

This is for all the teachers who carry work home every night and who are writing encouraging words to their students long after their own children have gone to bed.

This is for all the school secretaries who have put on more Band-Aids on skinned elbows than they have stamps on letters.

This is for every principal who had to have the courage to defend a teacher who was right for kids, or dismiss one who was wrong for them.

This is for every board member who drove home at midnight following a school board meeting and quietly kissed his own children as they slept and quietly prayed that something he approved tonight would make a difference in their lives.

And this is for every librarian who ordered a book for the school library and hoped that it added to a child's character and didn't detract from it.

And this is for every superintendent, as he sat alone in his office late in the evening after having to make a difficult decision, who truly understood the phrase "it's lonely at the top."

And this is for every teacher who understood the child who was different—in his appearance, in his actions, in his academic abilities, in his home environment, in his loneliness.

And this is for every custodian who took the time to sit down with a child and simply listen.

And this is for every bus driver who stops long enough to lovingly help the disabled child get on the bus or who encourages the child with a hug or a smile who is having a problem.

And this is for all educators who know that the money is not the reason they do what they do, but that there is a higher calling and it is simply to make a difference in the life of a child.

And let's not forget the primary teacher who carefully and methodically pulls a child's tooth, then lovingly puts it in an envelope and dates it and seals it and puts a sticker on it and hangs it all around the child's neck so that it makes it home safely.

And there's the high school teacher who overlooks the colored hair and the bizarre clothes of a student, but looks into his heart and soul to reach him.

And this is for each of you, who almost unknowingly catch yourself praying for a child, because you know no other place to turn.

And just what it is that makes a great educator, a great teacher, or a great school administrator?

We all know that it's the person who loves children despite their runny noses and their lack of good hygiene. They do everything humanly possible to understand their students. They try to make up for broken homes. They try to stop abuse. They struggle with a legal system to remove children from deplorable conditions. They make new policies to strengthen laws for children. They continue their own education in order do a more effective job in the classroom. They silently wonder how they can teach any more concepts or take any more burdens.

It may not be the most glamorous job, but it's the most gratifying.

It may not be the easiest job, but it's the most invigorating job.

It may not be the most restful job, but it's the most rewarding one.

For of all the challenges in the world today, nothing compares to it.

Different backgrounds. Different challenges. Different abilities. Different races, religions, creeds, cultures, interests. Different expectations. Different hopes. Different dreams.

Yet we meet them all. And in spite of what some might think, dedicated educator is some of the last great heroes. They always have been. They always will be.

So this is for you. Those of you who go to work every single day of the week to give it all you've got. We'll probably never honor you enough. We'll probably never pay you enough. We'll probably never be able to measure the results of your labors.

But just for a moment, would you stop, hold your head high, and know that for each of you who care so deeply about our children, and their future, and their hopes and their dreams, this tribute is for you. To the vast majority of us, you are truly one of the few remaining heroes on earth.

Thank you for your understanding, for your patience, for your unbridled passion to make a difference.

No pedestal stands high enough, no accolades will ever be adequate, no rewards will ever be significant enough to repay you for your commitment.

And if you are ever given the award of "Educator of a Lifetime," I'll be cheering the loudest.

"Unless one has taught... it is hard to image the extent of the demands made on a teacher." —Silberman

❧

33

"A Security Blanket, a Gymnast, and a Kid Called Sarah"

"Children need strength to lean on, a shoulder to cry on, and an example to learn from."

—Author Unknown

I call her "Baby Sarah." The fact that she is now an adult doesn't change a thing.

Sarah was our third child, born eight years after Todd. For whatever reason, God chose to bless us with one more.

His thinking may have been that we needed to realize that every child is different. Each is unique. Each has his own strengths and weaknesses. Each is a rare gem.

Sarah was a typical little girl. She loved dolls and tea parties and teddy bears. Her "security blanket," noticeably pastel green and yellow, went everywhere with her. The blanket had been lovingly knitted and given to us at Sarah's birth by Mrs. Kathryn Barnes, one of the kindest and most beautiful individuals we've ever known.

That blanket went with us on camping trips, to church, to the grocery store, to the grandparents. It accompanied us on every vacation for years as we would go to the mountains or to the beach.

Once, in Eureka Springs, Arkansas, we had strolled with all three kids into virtually every shop for a half-mile or better. At the end of the street, Sarah was ready for a nap, and started looking in the stroller for her blanket.

At her first whimper, we realized immediately what had happened. The blanket had fallen out of the stroller somewhere along the maze we had just completed.

Sarah cried. Mom grieved. Le'Ann soothed. Todd laughed. And I just looked confused.

"We'll get you a new blanket," I said.

"Don't cry, Sarah, it's OK," Le'Ann comforted.

"We'll find it, Honey," Mom responded.

"You're cryin' over that stupid blanket?" Todd added.

Inside, we were all wondering how Sarah was going to handle such a trauma. After all, a security blanket, carried for years, is imbedded with more memories than the family picture box. Every stain, every pulled thread, every blemish has a memory. That blanket was such a vital part of Sarah's life that Karen and I had often discussed having it bronzed for her when she graduated. I was certain that she wouldn't give it up until then.

We turned, started retracing our steps as we headed toward the car a half-mile away. After a quarter-mile or so, we were convinced that we had seen that beautiful yellow and green treasure for the last time.

All of a sudden, we heard a shout from Todd.

"I see it. I see it. It's hanging on that post up ahead. I see it!"

Sure enough, someone had picked it up, draped it over a fence post, and left it for us.

I'm almost certain that I saw a ray of heavenly light shining down on it as we all stood around the post, looking at Sarah's most treasured belonging, none of us speaking a word.

Finally, Le'Ann gently removed it, and handed it to Baby Sarah.

She stopped crying, smiled, took the blanket, shut her eyes, and went sound asleep.

"It's nothin' but an old blanket," Todd said. "I had already decided I'd jes'git her anuther one."

Yep. Each child is different. Each is unique. Each has his own strengths and weaknesses. Each is a rare gem.

❧

Sarah was a child who did her homework without being told. She actually wanted to go to church. She made good grades. She made good choices.

However, geography was never her thing. Several years ago, geography seemed to take a backseat to history. Schools stopped teaching about countries and their locations. Social studies classes virtually ignored it. For a while, at least, geography became a thing of the past.

That became evident one evening when Sarah was watching the winter Olympics with Le'Ann and our son-in-law, Brent. At the time, Sarah was in her second year of college.

The television showed gymnasts who were cavorting and spinning and flipping as if it were perfectly natural. They made it look so easy.

One particular gymnast was extraordinary. The audience was spellbound as she performed feats so flawlessly that it literally took your breath away. No one spoke a word as she did the seemingly impossible with ease and grace.

As she finished her spectacular routine, Brent asked, "She was unbelievable! Did anyone hear what country she is from?"

Sarah immediately offered her assistance. "What a silly question. It was printed right there on the back of her outfit."

"It was?" Brent questioned.

"Well, yes," Sarah said confidently. "Didn't you see it? She's from some little country called *Samsung!*"

❃

I've often wondered if the conversation would have flowed any differently if Panasonic or Sony had been posted on her back.

Priceless moments. Comments that will be told over and over again at family gatherings. Remarks that were made so casually, yet will be embellished and enhanced for generations.

It's so true. Each child is different. Each is unique. Each has his own strengths and weaknesses. Each is a rare gem.

And thank God, they are!

❃

34

"The City Girl Becomes a Country Gal"

❧

"The difference between the right word and the almost right word is the difference between lightning and the lightning bug."

—Roy L. Smith

O ur oldest daughter Le'Ann has always been our most creative one. She loves to decorate. Enjoys arts and crafts. Has gorgeous penmanship. Is organized. Was an exceptionally good student.

You get the picture. She was every teacher's delight. Neat. Studious. Polite.

A real teacher pleaser.

But, like each of us, she's better at some things than she is at others.

She and Brent had just moved their family from the very populated, very "yuppie" area of Grapevine-Colleyville, Texas, to a rural community some thirty miles west of Fort Worth. Springtown, Texas offered them everything they were wanting: country values, trees, space.

The country home they purchased was on three to four acres. It's laden with wildlife. Deer, raccoons, wild turkey, skunks, opossums, and rabbits are quite plentiful.

Almost anyone you talk to in Springtown will tell of seeing a deer or a wild turkey.

"They're everywhere," her new friends told her. "Just look for them."

Le'Ann had arisen early to begin the day. A hearty country breakfast seemed to be just the medicine her husband and three children needed. Eggs. Bacon. Toast.

It was another beautiful morning in the country, with the fresh air blowing gently through the kitchen window, and the tantalizing smells of breakfast were almost too much to handle.

As she glanced out her window, she couldn't believe her eyes. For there, perched on the cedarpost fence, was the biggest bird she had ever seen.

"Oh, my gosh, it's a wild turkey!" she almost shouted.

She couldn't wait to show the children. She had to let them see what everyone had been telling them.

Rushing into their bedrooms, she told each one to wake up and follow her. She retrieved her husband from the bathroom.

This was just too good!

"Now, be really quiet," she cautioned as they made their way to the kitchen.

Once there, each child was lifted to the kitchen counter, and given a perfect view of the welcomed visitor.

"It's a turkey! A wild turkey! Can you believe it! He's come to visit us this morning!" she shared.

She and the three children stood staring, mouths hanging open.

It was a sight to behold.

After a few moments of sheer wonder, her husband Brent leaned over and quietly announced.

"Le'Ann, that 'turkey' would be a *buzzard*."

The laughter started from Brent, who started the children giggling, and finally, the city girl who had moved to the country, joined in.

Distracted by all the laughter, the "turkey" looked toward the house, appeared to be shaking his head in disbelief, and flew off just as the sun was coming up over the horizon.

Oh, Le'Ann is neat. She's organized. She's creative.

But apparently no one ever took the time to teach her the difference between a wild turkey and a buzzard.

If I'd known the difference myself, I would have taught her.

But then, I wouldn't have this memorable story to recall each time I see a buzzard.

And quite frankly, I think it's a mistake that any of us could have made.

But more than anything else, I hope you discover it before it's on your Thanksgiving table.

❧

35

"Oh, the sound of children!
Such strength for my soul."

*"A person begins to show his age at about the same time
he begins to show pictures of his grandchildren."*

—Author Unknown

I paused just long enough to listen to the grandchildren. All of them. We were in the backyard and they were being their usual selves. It seemed that everything out there interested them. They watched a hummingbird. They played with a worm. They blew dandelion seeds. They discovered colorful small rocks in the driveway.

Children are such amazing little creatures!

It has occurred to me that there are certain times in one's life when you no longer have children around you.

For those of us in the education business, it happens when we take that better-paying job at the central office. No more kids around.

Or perhaps it's when you retire after teaching for thirty years. No more children every day.

It happens to those of us who are parents when we suddenly become "empty-nesters." And like a jolt from a stun gun, we realize they're gone. No more children around.

When we become grandparents, you realize it about thirty seconds after the car pulls out of the drive. You've had them for a few days, and now they're gone until that next visit. The laughter of children is gone again.

I was recently invited to be the guest speaker at the commencement service at the Gatesville Correctional Institution for Women. I'll admit it: I was a little apprehensive. I didn't know what to expect. This was new territory for me.

In case you aren't aware, schools in the state's correctional institutions are part of an unusual district known as the Windham Schools. Their "campuses" are located inside each unit in Gatesville, Huntsville, and other Texas correctional institutions. The district was established in 1969 by the Texas Legislature and is named after James Windham of Livingston, a 24-year member of the Texas Board of Corrections.

Talk about challenges! With little funding, few incentives for teachers, and out-dated facilities, these remarkably gifted, caring educators turn helplessness into hopefulness almost every day.

On this day, close to ninety of the inmates had successfully completed their work in order to receive their General Equivalency Diploma. The event was held in a chapel behind tall chain-link fences, lined with razor-sharp barbed wire.

As my assignee accompanied me across the grounds into the chapel, a nice crowd of visitors had already gathered. From all appearances, it could have been in any chapel in the country. The guests were nicely dressed, and obviously excited about their daughters, or wives, or mothers, or friends reaching this milestone.

As I took my seat on the stage, I was told that each graduate was allowed to invite two adults and as many children as they had. That explained the large number of children in attendance.

Promptly at 10:00 a.m., the familiar strains of "Pomp and Circumstance" began being played. Almost immediately, the graduates started marching toward the front of the chapel. In place of colorful flowing gowns and mortarboards, they were wearing the traditional white shirts and pants. An armed guard stood in front of each stained glass window.

I couldn't help but think what an unusual sight this was!

As the last inmate took her place, the music ended. In spite of all the efforts to make everyone comfortable, there was a feeling of uneasiness in the air.

A principal rose and walked to the podium. She took a moment to survey the room. A smile came across her face. Then, in a soft gentle voice, she began to speak.

"Ladies and gentlemen, we are so thrilled and honored to have you here today. We have been looking forward to this time for months. The ladies being honored today have worked long and hard in order to be a part of this ceremony.

"I notice that there are a great many children in attendance. As you can see by looking around, we're rather crowded in this small chapel. So, would those of you who are responsible for the children, do me a favor? We all know that sometimes children will cry or make a little noise, so if that happens..."

There was a momentary pause.

"Uh, oh. Here it comes," I thought. "Please, please don't ask them to leave. Please don't hurt these loved ones anymore than they have already been hurt. Just let these children make all the noise they want to. It won't bother me..."

"If that happens," she continued, "please don't worry about it. You see, we don't ever hear the sound of children around here... and we need it."

Almost immediately, the uneasiness left the chapel. The guests smiled and chuckled softly. The children who understood the remark had a surprised look on their faces. The guards looked at each other shrugged, and smiled. Visiting grandmothers and mothers dabbed their eyes to keep the mascara from running.

But the most obvious reaction came from the graduates. Many of them had tears in their eyes as they bit their lips to hold back almost unbearable emotions.

Sure, they missed their freedom. They missed shopping. They missed their family on the outside. But perhaps more than anything else, they missed the sounds of children.

For those are the sounds of hope, of optimism, of joy, of carefree days. It's better than any tranquilizer. It's more powerful than any sermon. Its impact can even reach the heart of those behind barbed-wire fences.

So today, stop and appreciate the sounds of children whenever you can.

For now I know that there is no sadder line in the world than I heard that day behind the walls of the correctional facility in Gatesville, Texas.

"You see, we don't ever hear the sound of children around here... and we need it."

❧

36

"The Forgotten One"

❧

"A good exercise for the heart is to bend down and help another up."

—Author Unknown

I'm going to tell you before I begin, that the names have been changed. The setting, the ages, the details, are not important. But you've all known this kid.

She came from what has become a typical home. Dad worked. Mom worked. Money was scarce. When she and her brothers and sisters were very young, they stayed after school with whoever was keeping kids in their home at the time. Usually there weren't any references.

"Poor people sometimes have poor ways," my Mom always said.

No one really paid a great deal of attention to her as she began to grow up. She'd wait alone after school until someone came.

She loved school. She loved to read. She always had a smile. And that golden, naturally curly hair was a knockout.

Such potential.

At the school play in second grade, she arrived at the last minute. Her hair wasn't combed, so just minutes before the curtain went up, her teacher pulled her aside and lovingly made futile attempts to improve an impossible situation.

No parent joined in the applause after her brief solo. Mom and Dad were out "doing their thing."

The assistant principal and I sat with her in the foyer of the school that evening and poured out compliments on her performance until a car pulled up in front and a horn sounded.

We walked her into the night air, and as we opened up the back seat, she brushed aside fast food wrappings and trash into the back floorboard. It joined beer cans, cigarette wrappers, and unpaid bills.

"Why the hell weren't you waitin' out here like I told you too," he growled.

As they drove away, we both stood silently and watched until the smoke from the exhaust had long since dissipated.

What a beautiful little girl. What possibilities. But so much to overcome.

As she grew older, she gradually began to lose her smile. Her grades began to drop. She didn't have the right clothes, because her wardrobe was purchased piece by piece at garage sales around town.

Nothing matched, and on most days, there were snickers behind her back.

While other students enrolled in dance, and soccer, and cheerleading mini-camps, she could only imagine.

In middle school, she started receiving some attention. Older boys with ideas of their own started passing the compliments, the half-cocked smiles, and the cheap thrills.

To be accepted by this new set of "friends," she started smoking. The natural brunette returned to being a blonde. The clothes that had always been too small had now become an asset in her mind.

She added tattoos and body piercing. Her time walking the streets began to increase; her time in school began to decrease.

In high school, she quit coming altogether, because it's difficult to go to school and care for a baby at the same time.

❧

At this point, our story stops momentarily.

After I wrote the above scenario, I asked various acquaintances to identify the young girl I had described.

"I know exactly who it is," one said. "It's Stacy. Stacy Hetzel."

Another said, "No doubt about it. It's that little Johnson girl, Wendy Johnson."

Still another, "I've thought about her a lot over the years. What ever happened to Jennifer?"

To be perfectly honest with you, it's none of the above, yet all of the above. The young lady I described is in every school in America. This fall, she'll start school in your kindergartens. She'll attempt to fit in with the other students in your intermediate grades. She starts getting noticed in your middle schools. She'll be seen less and less in your high schools as her grades drop and her interest outside of school increases.

But if you're at the right place at the right time, you'll meet her again.

She'll come walking in the front door of your elementary school and she'll tell you that they just moved into town, and she needs to get her little girl enrolled in school.

"Got one of those free lunch applications?" she'll reluctantly ask. "I could sure use it."

And she'll introduce you to her little blonde-headed girl who is all smiles and eager to learn.

"Honey, Momma will be out front after school. I may be a bit late, but you stay right here until I pick you up."

And out the door she goes.

And the forgotten child starts the cycle all over again.

❧

Oh, how easy it would be to stop right there. But it's doesn't have to end there. The cycle doesn't have to continue. Unquestionably, we all have seen the other side of the story as well.

We've all seen a similar little boy or girl who broke the cycle because a teacher took the time to encourage.

We've witnessed the results of a principal who took difficult steps in order to pull a child from deplorable conditions.

We've seen grades improve because a student experienced success due to a teacher who developed a relationship first and a reading assignment later.

We've seen changes that appeared hopeless, yet happened because an educator instilled hope.

So as we prepare to begin another year, may our focus truly be on the "basics." In addition to instruction, let's give them encouragement. In addition to homework, let's give them hope. In addition to remediation, let's give them a role model. In addition to lessons, let's give them love.

And then, perhaps *only* then, will the forgotten child become the one we most remember.

❧

37

"All French Fries are Not Created Equal"

"I don't necessarily agree with everything I say."

—Author Unknown

I had just completed a workshop in Oklahoma, and several of us went to eat at a local restaurant.

It wasn't long before the conversation turned to humor from children, one of my favorite topics.

The superintendent had been relatively quiet, but once this topic opened up, he jumped right in with his favorite grandchild story.

He related how his granddaughter loved to eat at McDonald's. While the kid's meal was always the order of choice, those french fries were her favorite.

She consumes hers, ask if she could take a few of everyone at the table, and often, another order for french fries would find itself in front of her.

No doubt about it: this kid *loved* french fries.

During one of those very special family events, the group visited an upscale restaurant.

Once seated, the menus were distributed.

Immediately, the little girl began asking, "Do they have french fries? I want french fries!"

The waiter assured her that they had french fries.

The price tag wasn't the same as at McDonald's, but they had french fries!

When the meals were delivered to the table, the little girl began to squeal with delight at the french fries she spotted on the tray.

"O-h-h-h-h! They're huge," she shouted.

Everyone waited patiently until each had been served.

"Time to eat," she announced.

She took a big bite, smiling from ear to ear, and then suddenly got this terrible expression on her face.

"Yuk!" she shouted. "These french fries are horrible. U-g-g-g-h! They taste like *potatoes!!!!*"

38

"Time: the Most Valuable Gift You Can Give a Child"

"The frightening thing about heredity and environment is that parents provide both."

—Author Unknown

It had been planned for weeks. The mother and the five-year-old daughter would spend the day together.

Two parents. Three children. And the mom and dad realized the benefits of spending time individually with their children. It had become a routine practice… and a good one! She and her husband both realized the benefits of spending time with their children. The father often took the son on such an excursion.

Mom and daughter left early. They arrived just as the stores were opening at the recently remodeled mall. They leisurely shopped. They ate at the five-year-old's favorite fast-food restaurant. They talked. And they laughed.

The mom used these days as an opportunity to devote full-time to her golden-haired daughter. This would be a day like many others before and many more to come that would be treasured for a lifetime.

Excitement reigned throughout the day. They tried on silly hats and modeled for each other. They spent an hour or more in the bookstore. Mom would point out the children's books that had been her favorites when she was a child. The little girl finally settled on her favorite and the mom and daughter jointly selected a book for each of the other two children.

"It's better to give than to receive," the mother casually mentioned.

This shopping trip was good for both mom *and* daughter. The growing family had recently moved to the country, where the air was clean and the stars could be seen at night. Traffic jams were practically non-existent in the rural area, and the few acres of trees and sunshine provided an ideal spot for the children to run and play.

As a result, an occasional trip into the "big city" was a real treat. It was no longer a regular routine to shop in malls and eat in fancy restaurants.

Around mid-afternoon, they loaded their purchases and their tired feet into the car. It would take at least an hour to drive home.

By this time, the little daughter was more talkative than ever. Her insight and her comments amused the mother as they headed toward the outskirts of the city.

"Mom, now that we've moved to our new town, am I going to get to take dance like I did at our old house?"

"Honey, I'm sorry, but there's no one in our new little town who teaches dance anymore. One of the ladies at church said that the lady who used to teach it had retired. She's not doing it any longer."

"Oh, OK," the five-year-old said, then lapsed into silence.

A few moments later, she asked, "When do I start gymnastics again?"

"Honey, I checked, but I wanted you and your little sister to be able to take that together, but they don't accept children as young as she is. Do you still want to go ahead and do it by yourself?"

"No. No, that would upset Annie to be left out. I'll wait until we can do it together."

Again, silence in the front seat.

"Do they have museum school where we live now? Remember, I used to go to that once or twice a week."

"I know you seemed to enjoy that, but there aren't any museums where we live now. It's too far to drive to do that. Are you terribly disappointed?"

"Oh, no. I always thought it was more fun when the whole family would go to the museum anyway."

A few moments later, she casually commented, "Well, I guess I'll have to do soccer then."

"Well, I'm sorry to have to tell you this, but we moved too late for signup. They did that last spring. We'll have to wait now until next season. You OK with that?"

"Sure," she responded. "I got sorta' tired of hearing a lot of the parents yelling at us. You didn't do that, did you, Mom?"

"Well, maybe a time or two," Mom admitted, "but I didn't like that either. I thought some of the parents got a little carried away."

"They sure did!" she quickly responded.

They drove a few miles in silence. The mom began to wonder if they'd done the right thing. The move had brought many new opportunities for the family, but such classes and lessons and activities were limited in this new area.

The little child sat there quietly, then finally said, "Well, what am I going to do this year?"

Almost without hesitation, the mom said, "Well... uh, I guess you'll... uh, you'll just have to spend more time with me."

The five-year-old pushed forward as far as the seat belt would allow. She turned toward the mother. Her eyes opened wide. The eyebrows raised. The smile immediately spread across the face.

She gave only a one-word response as she clinched her right fist, bent her elbow, turned the fist upward and brought it down along her side in a quick motion

In sports-like fashion, she shouted: *"YES!"*

❧

The mom in the story is our oldest daughter Le'Ann. The five-year-old is our granddaughter Haley.

And yes, the incident really happened.

It made me realize once again just how important it is to spend quality time with our children. Time and time again, troubled youngsters angrily remark that the mother or the father or both had no time for them. Children are often placed in so many structured activities and meetings and classes that their weekly schedule rivals that of a corporate executive.

I recall reading a story once of a dad who reluctantly took off work one summer day to take his son fishing. Both the father and the son recorded their thoughts that evening in their personal journals.

The dad wrote: "Took my son fishing all day. This has been one of the worst days of my life."

The son wrote: "Dad took me fishing today. This has been the happiest day of my life."

Students in our classrooms need the same thing. They need to feel that they are special in someway. They need to know that teachers and counselors and principals are there for them. They need to know that they're not just a number, but someone you care about.

Time. It's a funny thing. We've all got the same amount each day. But how we use it can vary greatly.

Some waste it. Some spend it wisely. Some use the bulk of it on themselves. Others share it generously.

Time. What a difference it can make for a young person. Spending your time on a child can turn failure into success. It can turn loneliness into companionship. It can bring hope to the hopeless.

A young successful attorney once said: '"The greatest gift I ever received was a gift I got one Christmas when my dad gave me a small box. Inside was a note saying, 'Son, this year I will give you 365 hours, an hour every day after dinner.' My dad not only kept his promise," he said, "but every year he renewed it and it's the greatest gift I ever had in my life. I am the result of his time."

Time. Giving it to a child might just be the best investment you'll ever make.

❧

"If I had it to do over again"

"*Choose a job you like and you will never have to work a day of your life.*"

—Confucius

"If I had it to do over again...."

How many times have we heard someone make that statement?

It seems to me that it's usually from older folks who have lived a good life, but somehow, can look back and see where they could have improved upon a situation. Not just for their own good, but for the good of others.

I, perhaps, fall into that category. Thirty years in public education is a long time in some respects; yet in others it was a flash. A dance that seemed much too fast. A rush through classrooms, and boardrooms, and offices that somehow today seems like one big blur.

What would I do differently? In reality, probably very little. But in my heart and soul, I'd like to think I'd do many things much, much differently.

If I had it to do over again, I'd spend more time listening to students. As someone wisely said, "Talking is sharing, but listening is caring."

If I had it to do over again, I'd eat less in the lounge, and more often in the cafeteria with the students. That's when you really learn who they are.

Every elementary student would have a "recess" during the day, and I'd run and play like a child for that brief time, for in every great teacher, there is a child who wants and needs to play.

If I could do it all over again, I would encourage more adults to come into the classroom. Not just parents, but senior citizens, disabled individuals, lonely people, different ethnic groups and others who would not only benefit themselves, but contribute so much to students. Perhaps then we would understand that while we are all different, we are so very much the same.

I'd not worry quite so much about laughter in the classroom, for we know that creativity begins to flourish when students are at ease in their environment.

If I had it to do over, during the first few weeks of school, I would discover at least one gift that every student possesses, then consider utilizing him or her when that gift could be spotlighted.

I would encourage students much, much more, and far more often, for through encouragement, amazing changes can begin to happen in the life of a student.

If I could do it again, I would make every effort to teach children the joy of silence, the benefit of solitude, and the incredible benefits of balance in one's life.

I would stress the importance of always doing our best, for we know that "every person's work, whether it be literature, or music, or pictures, or architecture, or anything else, is always a portrait of himself."

I'd introduce them to great literary works, to the beauty of classical music, to the works of the great masters. And I would remind them that great works are still being done today.

I'd manage to work into my lessons the importance of honesty, the value of integrity, the joy of serving others, the worth of hard work, and the merits of a good reputation.

I'd do everything possible to instill in students a love for our country. I would have a fervor for freedom and a passion for patriotism, and I'd leave no doubt that it must never be taken for granted.

If I had it to do over again, I'd leave work on time several days during the week. I'd use some of those precious hours to spend more time with my own family. Some of them I would use for myself, and I'd take a walk in a park, stroll along a stream, curl up with a good book, or visit an old friend.

If it were possible to do it again, I'd write more notes to my students telling them of their potential. For many students, it might be the only validation they ever receive that anyone cares.

If I had it to do over, I'd take more pictures of my students, I'd save every uplifting note they gave me, and I would encourage them to keep in touch.

I'd attend fewer school-related meetings and instead, spend that time watching my students as they participated in sporting events, and recitals, and other important functions.

I'd give less homework and encourage families to turn off the TV and turn on the joy of watching and listening to each other.

If I could do it again, I'd speak only positive words about schools, and teachers, and principals, and superintendents and board members. I'd work diligently to get all of them working together for the good of children. How surprised they might be to learn that they are all on the same page when it comes to impacting the lives of children.

And I would adopt the following statement as my eleventh commandment: "They don't really care how much you know until they know how much you care." What a life-changing, powerful statement!

And, if I could start over, I'd pray for each of them, regularly, by name. Prayers have made a tremendous difference in my personal life. Why wouldn't it make a difference in the lives of those I have been given to serve?

I'd strive to be a better role model, a better friend, a better teacher. I'd relish every moment I had been given to impact a child's life and perhaps change it forever. I'd be more grateful for the opportunity to participate in one of life's great rewarding works.

And then, only then, would I look back and say, "If I had it to do over again… *I wouldn't change a thing!*"

❧

40

"My Dream for Our Children"

"Fear not tomorrow, for God is already there."

—*Author Unknown*

S everal years ago, I was moved to tears upon hearing Dr. Martin Luther King deliver his now famous "I Have a Dream" speech. Following that speech, I was struck with the awesome reality that we should all have dreams, visions and hopes for a better world. Since the education of young people has been my life for over thirty years, I felt compelled to "dream" my own dream about the hopes and aspirations for our children. It is an awesome responsibility, but one that the world must accept and strive for if our greatest resource, our children, are to continue to be our world's greatest hope.

❧

My dream is that someday *all* parents will realize that they are their child's first and most important teacher.

I dream that someday the politicians will realize that diplomas are our most effective defense for world peace and understanding and that one day, this nation will begin to place the education of our children as the number one priority.

As the bumper sticker says, "I hope I live long enough to see the war department have to have a bake sale."

My dream is that one day we'll pay educators more than we pay our football players, and more than we pay our wrestlers, and rock musicians, and movie stars, and yes, even our baby sitters.

Oh, if only we paid educators what we pay our baby-sitters! For example, if we paid a teacher five dollars an hour for 22 students on the roll, they'd be making $110 an hour! And, at eight hours per day, it would equate to an annual salary of approximately $154,000!

I wish we *did* pay them as well as our baby-sitters!

My dream is that one day the world will recognize the fact that *every* child needs to be given an opportunity for an education.

Our schools in this country take *every* student, not just the elite, and unlike some foreign schools, we welcome every child whether he has a high IQ or not.

My dream is that one day kids won't have to go to bed at night crying because they're not sure if one or both parents will be there when they wake up.

I dream that one day kids will get as excited about reading as they are about Nintendo.

I dream that one day parents will turn off the television set at dinnertime and families will once again eat together, talk together, laugh together, and share together.

I dream that one day kids will look at past generations and shake their heads in utter disbelief that drugs and their use were once commonplace.

I also dream that our children will grow up and realize that becoming a parent is one of the most important responsibilities they'll ever have.

I dream that children will learn the worth of laughter, for as it has been wisely written, laughter is "the music of the soul," "the best medicine," "the shock absorber that eases the blows of life."

My dream is that one day child abuse will not be tolerated in this country, and that no child should ever be subjected to mental or physical abuse.

I dream that one day children will be able to play outside without fear of abduction; that they can run, laugh, play, share and trust and not live in fear and that childhood pastimes such as sandlot baseball and tree houses and riding bicycles will be experienced by every child.

My dream is that moms and dads will recognize that *time spent with* their children is far more important than *money spent on* their children.

I dream that schools will offer children opportunities to grow, and explore, and sample, and that *then* our children will discover an area of work or service that is fulfilling and that utilizes their God-given gifts and talents.

My dream is that teachers, administrators, bus drivers, school secretaries, cafeteria workers and anyone who works with children will realize that it's not enough just to tolerate kids, you have to love them.

For the ability to work with children is not only a God-given talent, it's a privilege.

And those who don't love children will do both schools and kids a favor and get out of the profession.

My dream is that our children will realize that in spite of its flaws, America remains the greatest country in the world. America is worth defending and protecting and saving.

It is my dream that when the flag passes by, or children hear the National Anthem, they'll know they're perfectly normal if that tear swells up in their eye and that strange, unexplainable lump comes to their throat.

I dream that everyone can experience the heartfelt joy of hearing America's young sing *"from sea to shining sea, God shed His Grace on thee."* Nothing is more beautiful!

I dream that we'll not only teach children everything that we can about today's world, but that we'll instill in them a thirst for knowledge all the days of their lives, for we know that "of all our human resources, the most precious is the desire to improve."

I dream that one day, children all over the world will be as one and that adults will learn from them.

As we know, children are not born with prejudice, we teach it.

Children do not see each other as black or white, brown or yellow, they see each other as equals.

I dream that our children will say far more "I love you's," far more "I'm sorry's," and far more "thank you's;" that they'll give far more hugs, make far more visits to *their* parents, and spend more time getting grass stains while playing with their children.

I pray that you, too, have the same dreams, the same hopes, the same love for our children.

It will take all of us, working with one goal, one cause, one basic desire: to see our children become the very best that they can become.

And what is our most effective weapon to make this dream a reality?

Perhaps Albert Schweitzer said it best when he said: "Example is not the main thing in influencing others. It is the *only* thing."

So, may my example, and your example, be better today than it was yesterday, and better tomorrow than today.

❧

Bonus Section

A word from the author

Karen and I have been so pleasantly surprised at the response to this little book. Teachers, aides, superintendents, board members, parents, food service workers, support staff, and student teachers have read it and told us how much they enjoyed it.

One lady said that "it should be required reading of every teacher and parent."

Several school districts have ordered a copy for every retiring teacher.

And, I've written a note to most of them.

In fact, Karen and I have personally sold some 3500 books following speaking engagements... and virtually every book has included a personal word of encouragement that I have handwritten on the inside front cover.

I'm trying to do what Momma has said so many times over the years: *"Son, always do a little more than you have to!"*

Well, all Karen and I can say is "thank you!"

Thank you for buying the first edition and necessitating a second printing. We decided to give it a whole new look, because we wanted to include a bonus section that would give you even more "food for thought."

These extra three chapters were selected after much thought and deliberation.

The final one is a re-print of one of the most popular columns I've ever written for Texas School Business magazine. It will bring you up-to-date on Todd.

I never cease to be amazed!

Now, sit back, relax, read, and enjoy!

And, it is our prayer that each of you will continue to make "all the difference" in the lives of those you touch.

41

Kids, Chaos, and Canned Goods: A Christmas Memory

"Thank God for what you have,
trust God for what you need."

—Author Unknown

Oh, the spirit of Christmas. A time of giving, of sharing, of caring for your fellowman. A time to reflect and realize that some things never change.

Today, teachers are still overworked and underpaid, yet so miraculously rewarded in the most unusual ways.

Every holiday season I am reminded of my early days of being a fifth grade teacher. It was December 1967, and only two weeks until the glorious holiday season was to begin. Every student and teacher in the building was counting down the days.

On the first Friday of December, my fifth grade students and I started "the project." I had decided to decorate the room with an "old-fashioned" flair.

Granted, I realized after a short while that we had perhaps gone a bit overboard. Cranberries and popcorn were being strung in one corner of the room. Hand-made ornaments were being crafted in another area. One mom had agreed to help, but she decided to have the children make large reindeer from cardboard boxes to stand around the tree. Another mom had insisted on coming and helping the children to make kachina dolls, a popular doll of the Indians of New Mexico. Another offered to make a giant menorah.

One of the dads stopped by to pick up his child for a dental appointment and immediately agreed to bring a split-rail fence to separate the tree and the reindeer form the student desk area.

"Uh, whatever," I said. "Absolutely! Go for it!"

At this point, I quickly calculated, the students should have about a 4' x 4' area there in the center of the room for their desks.

As I tried to visualize the final product, I remember thinking, "This is going to look a great deal like a Goodwill store."

Oh well, the holiday season is all about "peace on earth, *goodwill* to men."

As you can imagine, the room was utter chaos. As I stood wondering which area needed me the most, I glanced over to the popcorn and cranberry department. It did not appear to be going well.

"Now, kids, "I said. "There should be no more that six of you over there on that project…and there are at least half a dozen!" Now we can't have that!"

The deadly silence.

Finally, one brave little soul said, "Mr. Jordan, six *is* a half a dozen."

"Oh, of course it is!" I laughed. What was happening to my mind?

"I could have told you that if you're gonna string popcorn, it needs to be about a week old," the director of kachina dolls said.

"I know that," I lied. "But this way, the children can eat freshly popped corn while we're working. Nothing worse than old popcorn."

"Humph!" She responded.

I gave her my best smile.

"I'll sweep before I go home this evening," I thought to myself.

About that time, an announcement came over the intercom reminding all the children to bring canned goods for the less fortunate. The principal indicated that there would be a pizza party in January for the room that brought the most cans.

"Bring those canned goods, kids. Let's win that contest!"

After another thirty minutes or so, the room was suddenly transformed into a showplace. I had to admit that it looked great. We really hadn't learned anything that would be on the standardized test, but what a great afternoon we had had.

I knew that for some of them, this would be the closest thing to a holiday celebration they would have.

A few days before we were to be dismissed for the holidays, it was announced that our class had won the canned good contest. Shortly thereafter, the principal came around and asked if I would help him deliver them after school.

That afternoon, we loaded boxes and boxes of canned goods into the back of his pickup truck and began the delivery.

The next thing I knew, he had pulled up in front of the little rent house where my wife, daughter, newborn son and I lived.

"Riney," he said, "the staff talked about it, and you're one of the neediest families in town. We're gonna leave some of these with you."

Normally, I'm not speechless, but all I could think about was how I had promoted this event, and now, *I* was the recipient. "But...uh, but, I don't think that I should..."

"Of course you should, Riney. Come on, we've got a lot of stops to make. Let's get your boxes unloaded."

And so it was, in the Christmas of 1968, the Riney Jordan family of Grapevine, Texas sat huddled in a little rent house and beamed at a cupboard filled with more canned goods than at any other time in their life.

Hominy! Fruit cocktail! Candied yams! Pumpkin! And one entire shelf with no wrappers!

Beautiful! Not a lot of meat, but beautiful just the same!

And now, whenever I'm asked to contribute to a canned food drive, I reach for the "good stuff."

Canned hams! Canned tuna! Canned chicken! And, yes, even Spam.

So this holiday season, gather your family around, have a joyous meal of hominy, fruit cocktail, and Spam...and be thankful.

For as you know, it's the simple things in life that are often the most cherished.

"The little things, memories ever dear,
Remembered forevermore,
For the little things of this world of ours,
Give us something worth living for."

-Leona Krefting

42

Making it a better world . . . in three simple steps

"If anyone speaks badly of you, live so none will believe it."

—Author Unknown

I just love it!

We all agree that too many of today's kids are rebellious. They don't seem to show the respect that we think they should. They don't appear to have any morals, or ethics, or values about them. And they're getting tattoos and listening to sounds that we can't begin to describe as music. Is there no end to it?

Parents blame the schools. And wouldn't you know it! Schools blame the parents.

Hey! Stop it! There's enough blame to go around.

Many of you who read this are school administrators. You are the superintendents who are responsible for entire school districts. You are the central office administrators who are responsible for programs and support staffs. You are the principals who are responsible for individual campuses.

Maybe, just maybe, it's time to evaluate our own individual role in all of this.

I'll be the first to acknowledge that there are a great many young people who are just remarkable. They follow the rules, they respect authority, they show good judgment, and they are as moral and ethical as anyone.

But for those students who don't fall into that category, we need to do something. I need to do my part... and you need to do yours.

As someone once said, "I was waiting on somebody to do something about it... and then I realized that *I* was *somebody*."

So, starting today, let's make a real effort to do just three things. Oh, of course there are a great many more that I could have added, but these will make a good start.

1. Be the best that you can be. This means morally, ethically, and spiritually. It means being exemplary. Our kids need role models... quality role models... those who are not afraid to stand up for that which is right and good. Vow right now that you are going to clean up your language, make a better impression, and improve your image. If you've been guilty of wronging someone, make it right... and forgive those who have wronged you. You know what you need to do. Just do it!

2. Personally help meet the needs of at least one student today. That's right. Get out of your office and go help a kid. We all know at least one. It might be as simple and easy as dropping by and checking on them and letting them know you care. An incredible feeling will envelop *you* the minute it's done... and I can promise you that the recipient will *never* forget it! So... just do it!

3. **Take care of your own family.** I know. I'm getting really personal with this one. But those of us in this business who love what we do often forget about those we love the most. Leave work on time today... and spend some quality time with your family. Your spouse will be speechless. Your children will be flabbergasted. Your grandchildren will be tickled to death. Family...it's not just a *good* thing; it's a *priceless* thing! Once again... just do it!

Well, that's it. Three little things that can help change the world... one student at a time, one school employee at a time, one family at a time.

"Let it begin with me, Let this be the moment now,
With every step I take, Let this be my solemn vow:
To take each moment and live each moment in peace eternally,
Let there be peace on earth... and let it begin with me."

—Lyrics by Sy Miller and Jill Jackson

43

It may take a while, but...
Never give up!

"Do what you love, love what you do and always do more than you promised!"

Author Unknown

His parents always knew he was smart... but in a different way.

He never played the typical school game well, yet if it was something in which he was interested, he did remarkably well. For example, he was always interested in machines. He was notably good at eye/hand coordination.

And one of his greatest gifts: he loved people!

And, as you might suspect, they loved him in return.

His math, reading, social studies, and science grades almost always reflected a "need for improvement." As you might suspect, he generally "forgot" to do his homework. If he did it at all, he generally lost it. His desk and his locker were classified as a "mess," and he spent a great deal of his school day "socializing" with other students.

Reading was one of his most difficult areas. He simply didn't enjoy reading. This grieved the parents because they loved to read. His two sisters read every book they were handed. But reading to this kid was something he just didn't grasp.

It started in kindergarten and continued for what seemed like an eternity. He didn't read when he started elementary school... and he wasn't doing much better when he started to middle school.

And while his parents were certainly frustrated, you can only imagine how frustrated *he* must have been.

Oh, there were the usual tests, and as a result of those scores, he was eventually assigned to special classes.

Getting through middle school was not without its frustration either. In fact, successes became even more of a rarity for the struggling young man.

There were the extra classes during the summer. There were correspondence courses. There were tutors. And while the older sister and the younger sister brought home the good grades and the accolades, this middle child often expressed his disappointment through anger and rebellion.

But, in spite of poor grades, incomplete assignments, and few successes, he graduated from high school one year later than originally planned.

He knew college wasn't in his plans at that point in his life, so he joined the military and had a four-year journey around the globe.

Then came marriage, a job in the operations division of a major airlines, and children of his own.

And then, almost sixteen years later, he's ready.

He's ready to read. He's ready to study. He's ready to try college.

And so you can imagine the joy when his parents get a phone call from their son who so rarely succeeded in school. You can imagine the thrill when they hear about his first exam in his first college course.

The parents happen to be dining in a restaurant when the cell phone rings. Their son, who is now a mature, conscientious 32-year old, tells them that he has just gotten home from his evening class. He has made a perfect score on his first exam. 100! You can tell from his voice that he is proud. You can tell that he is excited about the results.

And his parents? *"Oh, thank you, Lord! It's been a long wait... but well worth it!"*

The course that the young man is taking teaches participants everything they need to know about programmable logic controllers, or PLCs to those who understand them.

The student?

Our son, Todd.

And the reason I tell you about our son's recent success is so that you won't give up on a child, either. We didn't. His teachers didn't. And fortunately, he didn't either.

It may be a long time before some students are ready to learn, but when they are... look out!

A wise educational psychologist once told us, "Don't worry about Todd. He was just picked green. One of these days, he'll mature."

And she was right!

As the Chinese philosopher once said, "When the child is ready to learn, the teacher will come."

Way to go, Todd! Your Mom and Dad knew all along that you had it in you!

And now... you know it, too!

All the Difference

Acknowledgements

"When the Red Red Robin Comes Bob Bob Bobbin' Along;" Lyrics by Harry Woods

"Just Whistle While You Work;" Walt Disney Productions

"Darktown Strutter's Ball" Lyrics by Shelton Brooks

"Happy Whistler;" Lyrics by Don Robertson

"Camptown Races;" Lyrics by Stephen C. Foster

"America;" Lyrics by Samuel Francis Smith

"The Battle Hymn of the Republic;" Lyrics by Julia Ward Howe

"America the Beautiful;" Lyrics by Katherine Lee Bates

"Three Coins in the Fountain;" Lyrics by Styne/Chan

"You are so Beautiful;" Lyrics by Joe Cocker

About the Author

Riney Jordan is a former teacher, principal, school public relations director, and assistant to the superintendent over a 30-year period in a suburban school district near Dallas/Fort Worth. His school district honored him by naming him their "Teacher of the Year" (1968). His community honored him as their "Citizen of the Year" (1982). And the state recognized his work by passing a resolution honoring him as an exemplary Texan (1993).

His most recent honor includes being named the 2000 "Texas Key Communicator" at the joint conference of the Texas Association of School Administrators and the Texas Association of School Boards. He joins the likes of Dallas business man H. Ross Perot, Former Mayor of San Antonio Henry Cisneros, Undersecretary of Education Linus Wright, and former Texas Commissioner of Education Dr. Mike Moses.

Riney is a national speaker who regularly communicates his message of encouragement to schools, colleges, and civic groups emphasizing that "children don't really care how much you know until they know how much you care." His stories are filled with humor, yet are often touching and heartwarming. He has currently presented over five hundred keynote speeches and workshops across the country.

In addition to his regular feature in the prestigious *Texas School Business* magazine, Jordan has been published in numerous school journals and newspapers. He holds a bachelor's degree in Elementary Education from Howard Payne University and a master's degree in Public School Administration from the University of North Texas.

Riney and his wife Karen now live in the picturesque little central Texas village of Hamilton. They are proud parents of three children and seven grandchildren.

❧

To order additional copies of this book,
please visit our website at
www.rineyjordan.com

In addition to his book, you'll find
CD's, tapes, posters, and bookmarks
to provide motivation and inspiration.

❧